MY CAREER STARTED IN
MEHEBA
SETTLEMENT
A REFUGEE CAMP LOCATED IN
ZAMBIA

BAZIBUHE MUHABWA

My Career Started in Meheba Settlement a Refugee Camp located in Zambia
Copyright © 2024 by Bazibuhe Muhabwa

Tellwell Talent
www.tellwell.ca

ISBN
978-1-77941-752-7 (Hardcover)
978-1-77941-751-0 (Paperback)

TABLE OF CONTENTS

CHAPTER I 1

CHAPTER II..5

CHAPTER III 43

CHAPTER IV 77

CHAPTER V..87

CHAPTER VI.. 117

CHAPTER VII 129

CHAPTER VIII...147

CHAPTER IX 167

CHAPTER X..201

CHAPTER XI 209

A Heartfelt Appreciation To
My Mentors At UNHCR Solwezi 229

REFERENCES 233

CHAPTER I

ABOUT THE AUTHOR

Biography

County:	Congo DRC
Province:	South-Kivu
District:	Walungu
Village:	Tchankombo

Bazibuhe Muhabwa, affectionately known as Bazi, is a dedicated scholar and advocate who contributes to the settlement of immigrants and refugees. He graduated from NorQuest College with a specialization in Immigrants and Refugees and moved on to pursue a Bachelor of Professional Arts with a major in Humanities at Athabasca University. Throughout his academic journey, Bazi has demonstrated an unwavering commitment to advancing the welfare of immigrants, refugees, and marginalized communities.

Academic and Professional Pursuits

Bazi's educational journey commenced at NorQuest College in ESL classes in Edmonton, Alberta, Canada. After two years of studying, he moved into the Settlement Studies program, focusing on Immigrants and Refugees. This educational background equipped him with a strong foundation for understanding the complexities and challenges immigrants and refugees face in their new environments. It provided him with insights into the critical issues surrounding settlement and integration.

Continuing his academic journey, Bazi is now working towards a Bachelor of Professional Arts degree, majoring in Humanities at Athabasca University. This endeavour has allowed him to refine his knowledge and skills further, positioning him as a knowledgeable and capable advocate for the causes he holds dear.

Involvement in Research and Critical Thinking

Bazi's active involvement in research, group discussions, and lectures has played a pivotal role in honing his critical thinking abilities. These experiences have encouraged him to delve deeper into the intricacies of immigrant and refugee issues. His reflective skills have been sharpened, enabling him to approach these complex topics with a well-rounded perspective.

Diversity and Equity Advocacy

Bazi's engagement in various initiatives reflects his commitment to promoting diversity and equity. His experiences have equipped him with a unique set of competencies that are invaluable in advocating for the rights and well-being of marginalized communities in Canada and worldwide. He has worked with a diverse range of individuals, including older adults, youths, refugees, people with disabilities, the homeless, and Indigenous people. This extensive interaction has enriched his understanding of the unique challenges faced by these groups and has allowed him to provide more effective support and advocacy.

Building Lasting Bonds

Bazi has forged strong and lasting bonds with individuals and communities worldwide through his education and career. His connections extend to immigrant families, refugees, peers, and community members. These relationships have been instrumental in driving positive change within these communities. His ability to connect with people from diverse backgrounds has enhanced his effectiveness as an advocate for immigrant and refugee rights.

Recognition for Impact

Bazi's impactful contributions have not gone unnoticed. He has been the recipient of several prestigious accolades, notably including the John and Barbara Pool Family Award, the Shine Award, and the Jason Lang Scholarship.

Acknowledgment as a Change Agent

His tireless efforts to guide and support individuals navigating challenging terrain have profoundly impacted the lives of refugees, youth, and marginalized communities. Bazi's dedication to his cause was underlined by a heartfelt expression of appreciation, showcasing his deep commitment to assisting those in need.

Bazi's journey from NorQuest College to Athabasca University is marked by his commitment to improving the lives of immigrants, refugees, and marginalized individuals.

His academic pursuits, research involvement, and advocacy work have honed his skills and made a substantial difference in the lives of those he serves. Bazi's dedication and recognition as a change agent reflect his positive impact on the communities. In addition, Bazi's main objective during his college experience was to refine his skills for his second career. He previously worked as a child and youth care worker in the Meheba refugee settlement in the northwestern province of Zambia. Bazi has a natural talent for leading and connecting with people, and he finds great satisfaction in helping individuals of all ages overcome the challenges they face in their lives. Since he was young, he has always dreamed of working for the United Nations High Commissioner for Refugees (UNHCR). He achieved this goal in 2016 when he joined the UNHCR workforce stationed in the Meheba settlement in Zambia.

C H A P T E R I I

LIFE IN ORPHANAGE

Map of Africa and Location of Congo DRC

This map shows Congo DRC in red within the African map. As demonstrated in the picture, the country has been in endless war since its creation. It is rich in resources such as mining, copper, cobalt, gold, diamonds, coltan, zinc, mineral processing, and consumer products (including textiles, plastics, footwear, processed foods, and beverages).

Capital: Kinshasa

Let me take you back to when I was still living in my home village, Tchankombo, in Walungu. I can still smell my home village and all the memories are still with me today. I grew up with my older brother and I have three siblings. My father was a businessperson, and my stepmother was a house mom. I love her so much!

A Journey of Resilience: Growing Up as an Orphan from a Young Age

The tapestry of life is woven with threads of unpredictability, and individuals are sometimes thrust into circumstances beyond their control from the earliest stages of existence. I stand as proof to this truth, having experienced the trials and tribulations of growing up as an orphan. As a child, I found myself bereft of the loving guidance and protection of my mother, leaving me to traverse the tumultuous path of life with little more than determination and resilience as my companions.

This story gives you a glimpse of my life journey, which has lasted many years. I have enjoyed great success as an orphan in a world that can be tough and unforgiving, although I faced difficult problems.

My journey started when my mother wasn't there anymore. Her absence felt like a big hole in my life that I couldn't fill. Being an orphan is tough because you feel like you've been left behind, and I felt the same way. At first, it was really hard. I felt so lonely and sad because my mom wasn't there anymore. While other kids had their families, I had to deal with a world that was often harsh and difficult. Some nights, I cried myself to sleep, missing out on bedtime stories and comforting lullabies.

Yet, the human spirit possesses an innate capacity for resilience, a quality that often shines brightest in the face of adversity. With each passing day, I summoned the strength to confront the world's challenges head-on. The absence of parental figures prompted me to seek mentorship and guidance from other sources, be it teachers, friends, or community members who extended their support. Though distinct from the conventional parent-child dynamic, these relationships served as beacons of hope, providing me with valuable life lessons and shaping my perspective on the world.

My path, characterized by its highs and lows, was not without its moments of success. Every milestone reached and each challenge conquered owed their existence to my unwavering determination and the invaluable backing of those who had faith in my abilities. Education became my refuge, providing comfort and paving the way for a more promising future. Through my quest for knowledge, I unearthed my inner resilience and potential. The world that once appeared relentless gradually unveiled opportunities and possibilities, even in the face of the hardships I had endured.

My narrative is not one of pity but of empowerment. It's a story of resilience, where adversity serves as a crucible that molds the human spirit into a force that can withstand the harshest circumstances. My experiences as an orphan have shaped my character, instilling within me an unwavering determination, empathy for others facing their own trials, and a profound appreciation for the beauty that life can offer, even in the face of hardship.

As I recount the chapters of my life, I hope to inspire others who have faced or are currently facing similar challenges. To show them that even without traditional family structures, a journey of resilience can lead to a life filled with meaning, purpose, and the pursuit of one's dreams.

The Early Days

My journey began in early 1991, a time when life was markedly different from what we know today. I was born into a world of uncertainty, as my mother succumbed to a devastating illness when I was just a toddler. With her untimely demise, I was thrust into the harsh reality of orphanhood, a term that carried a heavy weight in those days.

I found refuge in a local orphanage in the absence of a family to call my own. These early days were filled with confusion, fear, and an overwhelming sense of loss. The absence of parental love and guidance left a void that no one else could fill, but the orphanage staff did their best to provide us with the essentials of life —shelter, food, and rudimentary education.

The Struggle for Identity

I became increasingly aware of the circumstances that had led me to the orphanage as I grew older. Questions about my heritage, my parents, and the life I could have had if they were alive constantly gnawed at my young mind. While I yearned for answers, the staff at the orphanage had little information to offer.

My struggle for identity was compounded by the societal stigma attached to being an orphan. In the early 1990s, orphans were often viewed with suspicion and pity, and their prospects in life were limited. This societal prejudice only fueled my determination to prove that my worth was not defined by my parentage but by my actions and choices. However, one of the lifelines I clung to during those formative years was education. The orphanage may not have been able to provide a nurturing family, but it did offer access to basic education. I seized this opportunity with both hands, recognizing that knowledge was my ticket to a better future.

Education broadened my horizons and instilled in me a *sense* of purpose. I discovered a passion for learning and a hunger for knowledge that would become the driving force behind my journey. Despite the odds stacked against me, I was determined to excel academically and prove that I could rise above my circumstances.

Life as an orphan was not without its hardships. I faced numerous challenges, including discrimination, poverty, and the constant struggle for acceptance. The road to success was fraught with obstacles, and there were moments when despair threatened to overwhelm me.

Conversely, during these trying times, I drew strength from my past and the lessons I had learned. I reminded myself that I had already overcome the greatest adversity—the loss of my mom. With that perspective, I faced each new challenge with renewed determination, refusing to be defined by my circumstances. As I entered adulthood, I found myself at a crossroads. Despite the odds, I completed my education and acquired valuable skills. It was time to carve out a path for myself and make a meaningful contribution to society. Driven by a deep desire to give back and make a difference, I decided to dedicate my life to helping other orphans and disadvantaged children—providing them with an education, support, and a sense of belonging to those in this unforgiving world.

Life with My Beloved Stepmother

Living a life of relative comfort and bliss, I resided contentedly with my mother, completely oblivious to the fact that she was not my biological parent. My early years were marked by innocence and a blissful ignorance of the complexities that lay beneath the surface of our seemingly ordinary family life. However, one day, as I looked through our cherished family photo album, I found a picture that changed how I saw my life forever.

In that photograph, I saw my father standing beside another woman. This woman, who held a young baby in her arms, was a stranger to me. Her features were distinct: she had long hair and a warm, brown complexion. Confusion coursed through me as I gazed upon this peculiar image. Who was she, and why was my father intimately poised beside her with his hand gently resting on her shoulder?

Driven by an insatiable curiosity that often accompanies childhood innocence, I ventured outside to seek answers from my stepmother. Brimming with questions, I approached her and inquired about the mysterious woman in the photograph. To my utter shock, my stepmother reacted with a swift slap across my face and a stern command to return the photo album indoors, never to lay my hands on it again.

This incident left me both envious and deeply intrigued. The woman in that photograph had become an enigma that I was determined to unravel. That singular photograph triggered a tumultuous period in my life, marked by a relentless rebellion against my stepmother. I became obstinate, refusing to heed her words and rebelling against her authority. Upon returning home from his work on the farms or at the market, my father was consistently greeted with tales of my incessant battles with my stepmother.

I found myself physically confronted and subjected to punishments, all to suppress my incessant inquiries about the woman in the photograph. It was a protracted period of turmoil, and I couldn't quite fathom why I was so consumed by the need to uncover the truth behind that image.

Strangely enough, I developed a peculiar habit during this tumultuous phase. Whenever I was provoked or subjected to punishment, I retreated to a personal sanctuary where I could cry alone. This refuge of mine was located behind our rural home. In our rural community, each plot of land offered ample space for cultivating crops and raising livestock such as cows, goats, sheep, chickens, and pigs. Behind our home, there was a small hill that stood out distinctly.

I cherished that little hill as a place to find solace and solitude. However, each time my father spotted me on that hill, his response was an escalation of both corporal and physical punishment. I was repeatedly warned never to set foot on that hill, yet I inexplicably continued to defy this simple and clear directive.

This became the second source of discord between my stepmother and me. The first was my relentless pursuit of information about the woman in the photograph, and now there was the mystery surrounding my visits to the hill. My stepmother possessed the answers to these questions, but for reasons unbeknownst to me, she refused to share them. Thus, the battles persisted, unrelenting over the years.

One fateful day, my uncle, perhaps sensing my overwhelming confusion and distress, decided to divulge a shocking revelation. He casually mentioned that the hill where I sought solitude was the very spot where my biological mother had been laid to rest. The weight of this revelation crushed me, leaving me bewildered and traumatized. I was still a child, forced to bear the heavy burden of this unsettling truth.

This revelation, in turn, became the third catalyst for my ongoing clashes with my stepmother. I couldn't comprehend why she had concealed such vital information from me, and so I confronted her. Unsurprisingly, my attempt to extract answers resulted in yet another brutal beating. I also sought answers from my father, only to be met with harsh physical punishment.

In retrospect, I was traumatized at a young age, grappling with questions about my mother's death and my true origins. I was consumed by a burning desire to unravel the mystery of my existence, to understand why I had grown up without my mother's love, and to ascertain the identity of the person responsible for her untimely demise.

My relentless pursuit of the truth led me to persistently question my father about the circumstances of my mother's death. Each time we found ourselves in a calm moment together, I seized the opportunity to inquire about her. I wanted to know what she loved most, who her relatives were, her aspirations for her children, and her favourite foods. These questions were my attempts to connect with her and carry her legacy forward somehow.

They say that "persistence pays off," and as I continued to ask these questions, my father gradually opened up. He must have felt that I was now old enough to comprehend the concept of death and my mother's passing. It took nearly a decade, but one day, he decided it was time to share the full story of my life with me.

My father sat me down with great solemnity and recounted every detail I needed to know about my past. He painstakingly pieced together the evidence and memories, ensuring that I grasped the profound complexities of my dark and mysterious background. This conversation occurred nearly a decade after I had first stumbled upon that enigmatic photograph, marking a pivotal moment in my quest for understanding and closure.

Here is My Life Story

At a very young age, my father shared a remarkable story with me, one that highlighted the extraordinary circumstances of my early life. It all began when my biological mother responded to what she believed was a divine calling, and my maternal relatives made a difficult decision that would shape my future. They believed that my father's side of the family had somehow contributed to my mother's untimely death, so they entrusted my care to my dad.

At the time, I was less than four months old, and my father faced an immense challenge. Without my mother to provide me with nourishment, he had to find a way to ensure my well-being. In those desperate circumstances, an unconventional solution presented itself: I was to be breastfed with goat's milk. It was a decision born out of necessity and carried a significant risk.

As my father recounted this extraordinary tale to me, I couldn't help but be moved by the profound circumstances of my early life. The very beginning of my existence was marked by uncertainty and hardship. It was a time when the odds were stacked against me, and the unconventional choice of goat's milk became a symbol of the resilience and determination that would shape my life.

The decision to feed me goat's milk was not made lightly. It was the only option left and showed my father's love and dedication for me. He understood the gravity of the situation and was willing to go to great lengths to ensure my survival and well-being. It was a sacrifice he made without hesitation and a choice that ultimately saved my life.

As I grew older and heard this story more than once, it constantly reminded me of the strength and resourcefulness that defined my family. We had faced adversity head-on and found innovative solutions to overcome it. In those early months, goat's milk had sustained me, but my father's true love and determination truly nourished my spirit.

My father's narrative painted a vivid picture of the challenges we had overcome as a family. It was a story of love, sacrifice, and the unbreakable bond between a father and his child. It was a story that emphasized the importance of family and the lengths to which we would go to protect and care for one another.

The memory of those early days, with me being fed goat's milk, was a powerful reminder of how fragile life can be and how resilient the human spirit is in the face of adversity. It is a fact that unconventional solutions are sometimes necessary to navigate the most challenging circumstances.

As I tearfully listened to my father's words, I felt a deep gratitude for his sacrifices on my behalf. His love and dedication had carried me through those precarious early months, and they continued to guide me as I grew older. The story of goat's milk was a symbol of our family's strength and determination, and it reminded me that even in the most trying times, love and family could provide the nourishment we needed to thrive.

In many ways, that early chapter of my life laid the foundation for the person I would become. It instilled in me a sense of resilience and gratitude, teaching me that no matter the obstacles I faced, there was always a way to overcome them. It underscored the importance of family bonds and the power of love to conquer adversity.

As I reflect on that remarkable story my father shared with me, I am reminded that life often takes us on unexpected journeys, and our response to those challenges defines who we are. I am grateful for the love and determination that carried me through those uncertain early months, and I carry that gratitude with me as I continue to navigate life's twists and turns. My father's story is a constant reminder of the strength of the human spirit and the enduring power of love.

In May 1990, a ray of hope dawned upon my life, changing its course forever. It was a stroke of fate that brought an organization into existence, one that would prove to be the lifeline for children who had been orphaned, whether due to the loss of both parents or the tragedy of a single-parent household. This organization embarked on a mission to seek out these vulnerable children, offering them the prospect of a safer and more secure future. Little did I know that this benevolent institution would soon become my sanctuary, my refuge from the stormy sea of uncertainty.

At the time, my world was a small village called Tchankombo, where I resided with my father. Our circumstances were far from idyllic. The burdens of life weighed heavily upon us, and the prospect of a brighter future seemed like a distant dream. My father, driven by a deep love and concern for my well-being, decided to reach out to this organization for assistance. He believed they could provide me with the support and opportunities our modest life could not afford.

To our immense relief, the organization responded to my father's plea with compassion and generosity. They extended their benevolent hand and agreed to take me under their wing, offering me a chance to escape the harsh realities of our world.

This marked the beginning of a transformative journey, one that would shape the rest of my life in unimaginable ways.

The destination of this journey was a place called "Mugogo," a town that would soon become my new home. This remarkable organization had established a haven for children like me—a sprawling orphanage where we could find shelter, care, and, most importantly, a sense of belonging. As I embarked on the journey to Mugogo, I could not have fathomed the profound impact it would have on my life.

Stepping onto the grounds of the orphanage, I was greeted by a sight that filled my heart with both trepidation and hope. There were children from diverse backgrounds, each with their own stories of hardship and adversity. Yet, despite our varied pasts, we were united by a common thread—the yearning for a better future and the solace of knowing we were not alone in our struggles.

Over time, the orphanage became more than just a place of refuge; it became a second home and a surrogate family. The dedicated staff and volunteers worked tirelessly to ensure that we received the care, education, and emotional support we needed to thrive. They provided us with the tools to break free from the cycle of poverty and despair that had haunted our lives.

As I grew and learned within the nurturing environment of the orphanage, I discovered my own potential and developed a sense of purpose. My friendships with my fellow residents were bonds forged in the crucible of shared experiences. Together, we faced life's challenges head-on, empowering each other to dream, aspire, and believe in a brighter future.

Looking back, I realize that the arrival of that benevolent organization in May 1990 was nothing short of a miracle in my life. It rescued me from the clutches of a bleak existence, offering me opportunities that I could have never imagined. It transformed a young orphan into a person filled with hope, ambition, and a determination to make the most of the second chance that life had given me.

In the following years, I carried the lessons and values instilled in me at Mugogo as I ventured into the world. The support I received from that organization allowed me to break free from the cycle of poverty, pursue an education, and build a future that I could be proud of.

Today, as I reflect upon my journey from a small village to a life filled with possibilities, I am forever grateful for the organization that changed my life. They not only provided me with a safer place but also with the wings to soar. Their compassion and generosity have left an indelible mark on my heart, inspiring me to pay forward the kindness that was extended to me in my time of need. Ultimately, the power of love and empathy transformed a vulnerable orphan into a beacon of hope for others.

I lived in the Mugogo orphanage for nearly nine years. During that time, my fellow children and I shared the simple joys of childhood. We ate together, played together, and cherished the love that made up our days.

Yet, there was a rule at the orphanage that when a child reached the age of ten, efforts would be made to find their family or relatives so they could go to school and be with their loved ones once more. And so, as fate would have it, that moment arrived for me. I knew it was time to prepare myself to leave the orphanage behind.

In the days leading up to my departure, the atmosphere was filled with mixed emotions. Excitement for the future mingled with the sadness of saying goodbye to the friends I had grown so close to. The orphanage staff and children organized a grand celebration, a farewell of sorts, to send me off on this new chapter of my life.

The celebration was filled with laughter, music, and delicious food. It was a bittersweet occasion, as I felt deeply grateful for the care and love I had received at Mugogo. The memories I had created there would forever hold a special place in my heart.

As the day of my departure drew closer, I couldn't help but reflect on the journey I had taken at the orphanage. It had provided me with a safe and nurturing environment, but now it was time to reunite with my family and embrace the opportunity to receive an education.

Leaving the orphanage was both a challenge and a promise of a brighter future. With the support of the friends I had made and the memories I carried with me, I embarked on this new adventure, filled with hope, as I prepared to rediscover my roots and continue my journey in the world beyond Mugogo.

A Childhood in Transition: Leaving Behind the Only Family I Knew

Childhood memories are often a treasure trove of emotions etched in the deepest corners of our hearts. Some of these memories stand out as profound, life-altering moments that continue to shape our understanding of the world. One such moment in my life was the heart-wrenching experience of leaving the only family I had known for nearly nine years. It was a transition from innocence to reality, a transformation that challenged my perceptions of love, belonging, and identity.

The Comfort of Home

In the early years of my life, I found comfort and security in a place that I believed would be my forever home. My close friends often told me, "We love you, Bazi," and this affirmation of affection was a constant source of solace. It was a home filled with warmth and camaraderie, where the bonds we shared felt unbreakable. The white woman who cared for all of us children had become our mother figure, and the sense of maternal love she provided was genuine and unwavering.

Identity and Belonging

In my young and impressionable mind, I believed in the narratives that were woven around me. I thought my beloved brother named Debaba was my biological sibling, and our connection was as strong as any blood bond could be. The white man with the long beard, who was a prominent figure in our lives, was our father, or so I thought. The horses we rode every morning and evening, the very essence of our daily routine, were seen as an integral part of our family's legacy.

The Farewell

The day I had to leave this cocoon of love and comfort was one of the hardest and most bewildering moments of my life. As a child, I couldn't comprehend the reasons behind this separation. I remember the teary-eyed faces of my close friends, their voices quivering as they told me, "We will miss you Bazi." Those words still echo in my mind, a poignant reminder of the depth of our connection.

The Harsh Reality

Leaving behind the family I had grown to love and trust was my first encounter with the harsh realities of life. It was a jarring awakening to the complexities of identity and belonging. I realized that the white woman who had cared for us was not my biological mother, and the man with the long beard was not my father. The horses I had thought of as our own were not part of our family's heritage. The bubble of innocence had burst, and I was thrust into a world where the boundaries of love and family were not as clear-cut as I had once believed.

The memory of leaving the family I had known for the first nine years of my life still brings tears to my eyes. It was a vital moment that forced me to reevaluate my understanding of love, family, and identity. While it was a painful transition, it was also a valuable lesson in the complexities of human relationships. Reflecting on that challenging period, I am reminded that life's most profound lessons often come from the most unexpected experiences, shaping us into the individuals we are meant to become.

Leaving behind the familiar faces of the boys and girls I had grown up with was one of the most challenging things I've ever had to do. The memory is still so vivid in my mind, like a scene from a movie that plays over and over again. I can still feel the weight of those emotions as I hugged my Matron and Patron tightly, tears flowing freely down my cheeks.

The Matron and Patron had been like parents to me during my time at the orphanage. They had watched over me, cared for me, and provided me with the love and support I needed. They were the ones who guided me through my formative years, teaching me valuable life lessons and giving me a sense of belonging.

As I stood there, clinging to them, I couldn't help but feel the overwhelming sadness of leaving them behind. It was a bond forged over years of shared experiences and care. The tears that fell were confirmation to our deep connection.

But then, there was another twist in the story. My father, whom I hadn't seen for nine long years, appeared with a woman by his side. This woman was introduced to me as my mother, someone he had married during my absence. It was a moment filled with confusion and mixed emotions. How could this woman suddenly be my mother when I had known no other parents but the Matron and Patron in the orphanage?

Despite the introduction, I was far from convinced that I had a family beyond the orphanage's walls. It all felt surreal, like a dream I couldn't quite wake up from. The orphanage had been my world for as long as I could remember, and the Matron and Patron had been my parents. Accepting these new people as my parents was a challenge I wasn't sure I was ready for.

As the day wore on, it became apparent that there was no other option but to go with my father and mother. The journey back to what was now supposed to be my home was a two-day trek on foot, and the sun was already beginning to set. It was a difficult decision, one that seemed to leave me with no choice.

I remember both the Matron and Patron accompanying a group of people who had come to pick me up. It was a sombre procession, a mixture of emotions in the air. There was sadness in saying goodbye to the familiar faces of the orphanage, but there was also hope for a new beginning with my father and stepmother.

Right before we reached the gate that marked the boundary between my past and my uncertain future, Matron and Patron pulled me aside from the group. They knelt, one after the other, and kissed my forehead. Their gestures were filled with love and tenderness, and their words have stayed with me to this day.

"We love you so much, Bazibuhe," they said, their voices filled with emotion. "Keep on being a good boy. Your father and I will keep praying for you." My Patron added a piece of advice that would guide me through the years to come: "Respect these parents in your whole life; respect everybody, young or old. Demonstrate good behaviour, and then we will see you again."

Those words, spoken sincerely, cut through the sadness enveloping me. They were a reminder of the love and guidance I had received at the orphanage and a promise that I would carry their lessons with me wherever I went. But despite their words of encouragement, I couldn't find the right words to express the depth of my sadness and uncertainty.

Leaving behind the only family I had ever known was heart-wrenching. The faces of my fellow boys and girls from the orphanage were etched into my memory, and our bonds were unbreakable. They were more than just friends; they were my brothers and sisters and leaving them behind felt like tearing a piece of my heart away.

My Matron and Patron had been my pillars of strength. They had filled the void my absent parents left and given me the love and care I needed to thrive. Their presence had shaped my character and had instilled in me values that would serve as my guiding principles in life.

As I embarked on the journey to my supposed new home with my father and stepmother, I felt a sense of trepidation. The world outside the orphanage was vast and unfamiliar, and I was leaving behind the safety and security I had known for so long. My father and stepmother, despite being my biological family, were still strangers in many ways.

The journey itself was physically and emotionally gruelling. Two days of walking through unfamiliar terrain tested my endurance and resilience. But as I walked beside my father and stepmother, I began to see glimpses of the people they were beneath the surface. They shared their hopes and dreams for me, offering a glimmer of connection amid uncertainty.

Over time, I started to adjust to my new life. My father and stepmother did their best to make me feel welcome and loved. They shared stories of the years I had missed, filling in the gaps of my past. Slowly but surely, I began to see them not just as strangers but as my parents.

Yet, the memory of the Matron and Patron who had raised me never faded. Their lessons, their love, and their guidance were a constant presence in my life. I carried their words with me, a reminder of the values they had instilled in me. Their love remained a guiding light, helping me navigate the challenges of adolescence and young adulthood.

As the years went by, I made it my mission to honour the promises I had made to my Matron and Patron. I treated my parents with respect and kindness, just as I had been taught. I demonstrated good behaviour and worked hard to make them proud. It was my way of keeping the memory of my orphanage family alive and showing them that their love had not been in vain.

Through it all, I held onto the hope of one day reuniting with the people who had meant so much to me. The Matron and Patron had promised to see me again, and I clung to that promise like a lifeline. I knew that no matter where life took me, their love and guidance would always be a part of who I was.

And then, one day, that long-awaited reunion happened. Years had passed since I had left the orphanage, and I had grown into a young adult. I had pursued my dreams and worked hard to make a life for myself, but the love and memories of the orphanage never left me.

I received a message one day that the Matron and Patron were coming to visit. The excitement and anticipation I felt were indescribable. It was a moment I had longed for, a chance to see the people who had shaped my life so profoundly.

When they arrived, it was as if time had stood still. Their faces were etched with the same warmth and kindness I remembered. We embraced tightly, tears of joy and gratitude flowing freely. It was a reunion filled with love and shared memories, an attestation to the enduring bonds that had been forged in the orphanage.

As we sat together, catching up on the years that had passed, I reflected on the journey that had brought me to this moment. Leaving the orphanage was one of the hardest things I had ever done, but it was also a necessary step in my journey.

Memories are Never Forgotten

As we departed from the gate, my heart sank as I watched the gate door inching closed, an irrevocable separation unfolding before my eyes. It was at that poignant moment that the reality hit me like a sledgehammer—I was gone, forever removed from the only life I had ever known. Desperation gripped me as I continued to wave frantically at the slowly vanishing gate, desperately hoping that one of my beloved orphanage family members would rush to my rescue.

Unbeknownst to me, my friends, those dear companions with whom I had shared countless memories and formed unbreakable bonds, had already gathered to mourn my absence. Each of them expressed their grief in their unique way, tears flowing like a river of sorrow, their cries resonating with the deep sense of loss that had enveloped them.

In a cruel twist of fate, I found myself isolated, cut off from the comforting presence of my friends, and devoid of any means to communicate with them or reach out to my orphanage parents. The world around me had transformed into an uncharted, bewildering landscape, and I was left to navigate it alone, yearning for the familiar embrace of the people who had been my family for so long.

The most cherished and significant keepsake from my time in the orphanage was undoubtedly my Memory book. It held a special place in the hearts of every child living there, as each one of us had our very own Memory book. This seemingly ordinary book was a repository of our hopes, dreams, and a connection to the world beyond those institutional walls.

Within the pages of our Memory books, vital information about our potential family members was meticulously recorded. The names, addresses, and areas where they lived were carefully documented, offering us a glimmer of hope and a glimpse into our unknown roots. This information was like a lifeline for us, a connection to a family we had never known or met.

But our Memory books were more than just directories of potential family members. They were our personal journals, filled with stories, emotions, and memories that we held dear. We were encouraged to document our family connections and include the names of our closest friends. These friendships were the pillars of support in our otherwise uncertain lives, and their inclusion in our Memory books symbolized the importance of these relationships.

As time went on, our orphanage management added more layers to our Memory books. They became living documents, chronicling our growth, achievements, and experiences. Birthdays, holidays, and special moments were all recorded on those pages. Gradually, it transformed into a comprehensive life history detailing the milestones we had achieved and the challenges we had overcome.

Our Memory books served as a source of comfort and motivation for many of us. They were a tangible reminder of our identity, roots, and the people who cared about us. In those moments of doubt and loneliness, flipping through the pages of our Memory books provided solace and a sense of belonging.

Our memory books were more than just records; they were a reflection of our resilience and our unwavering hope for a brighter future. They held the power to connect us with our past and inspire us to dream of a better tomorrow.

These simple books became our shared journey, reminding us that even in the face of adversity, we could create lasting memories and leave behind a legacy of strength and courage.

Life in My Village

Arriving in Tchankombo, my newfound home, I was overwhelmed with mixed emotions. Nervousness seemed to wash over me, making me feel somewhat nerveless, as if I had no control over my own fate. This was a fresh start, a new chapter in my life, and it was intimidating. I felt like a stranger in a foreign land. The life I had known was left behind, and I wondered if happiness would ever find its way back to me.

One person, however, began to shine like a beacon of hope amid the uncertainty: my stepmother. She is an incredible woman; her warmth and kindness were like a lifeline for me. Her consistent care and the way she would look at me with affection made me feel cherished and protected. Every time she uttered those three powerful words, "I love you," it was as if she was building a bridge between my past and my present. Slowly but surely, she erased the doubts lingering in my heart.

Creating new friendships was a daunting task. I had to rediscover the art of making friends from scratch and navigating through the complexities of human connections. It felt like learning to walk again after a long period of immobility. But with my stepmother by my side, I gained the courage to take those first steps. She became my guardian and confidant, guiding me through the intricate web of social interactions.

I began to rebuild my life in the warmth of her love and the security of her care. Tchankombo, once a place of uncertainty, started to feel like home. I learned that home is not just a physical place; it's where you find love and acceptance. My stepmother, in all her wonderful ways, made me believe that maybe, just maybe, happiness could once again be a part of my life. She wasn't my birth mother, but her love was a force that transcended biology, slowly mending the broken pieces of my heart.

Besides that, living with my new family for all these years has been a journey filled with ups and downs, and it's safe to say that life has taken on a whole new meaning. It's been a rollercoaster ride of emotions, and I can't help but feel like I've been on a constant quest for answers to questions that seem to have no clear solutions. The sense of betrayal and confusion often creeps in, leaving me with a profound feeling of isolation and loneliness.

One of the significant events that shook my world was the recent passing of my father. The loss of a parent is an indescribable pain that transcends words. It leaves an emptiness that is challenging to fill. As I navigated through the complexities of life without my biological father, I began to understand just how bewildering it can be for anyone in a similar situation. The absence of a biological parent creates a void that is hard to comprehend, and it forces you to redefine your sense of self and family.

One thing I've noticed during my journey is that life's challenges are even more pronounced among orphans and children today. It's disheartening to see how they often bear the brunt of poverty. Without their parents' loving guidance and support, they face a daunting uphill battle in pursuing their dreams and aspirations. The dreams that should be soaring high seem to be grounded by the harsh reality they face daily.

Poverty's grip on orphans and disadvantaged children is relentless. It's not just about the lack of material possessions; it's about the limited opportunities, the missed chances, and the constant struggle to break free from the cycle of hardship. For many of them, the future can feel like an elusive dream that keeps slipping through their fingers.

The absence of parental guidance and emotional support can take a heavy toll on a child's well-being. It's in those moments of solitude and uncertainty that loneliness becomes a constant companion. It's difficult to convey the isolation that comes from not having someone to confide in, someone to share your dreams and fears with. The absence of clear answers to the questions that plague your mind can make you feel adrift in a sea of uncertainty.

But there is hope amidst all the challenges and heartaches— hope that stems from the resilience of the human spirit, the kindness of others, and the power of community. It's the hope that these orphaned and disadvantaged children can still reach for the stars and make their dreams come true with the right support and opportunities. It's the hope that despite the odds, they can break free from the shackles of poverty and loneliness.

In my own journey, I've come to realize that family isn't just about blood relations; it's about the people who love and care for you. It's about finding hope in the arms of those who embrace, support, and guide you through life's challenges. It's about the bonds we create and the strength we draw from each other.

So, as I continue to navigate the complexities of life with my new family, I hold onto the hope that even in the face of adversity, we can find the answers to our questions, the warmth of companionship, and the strength to overcome life's obstacles. And I believe that with love, support, and determination, every child can find their path to a brighter future, no matter their circumstances.

How Does Poverty Limit the Possibilities for Orphan Children and Youth to Realize Their Rights?

Children hold the future of our society in their tiny hands. How we nurture and care for them today will shape the leaders and citizens they become tomorrow. Unfortunately, throughout history, children have often been overlooked, undervalued, and treated as if their voices didn't matter. This mistreatment has been particularly evident in the case of orphaned children or those living in orphanages.

In many societies, children, especially those in orphanages, were once regarded as insignificant, voiceless beings who contributed little to the broader community. This harsh reality meant that their needs were often disregarded, and their potential was left untapped. These children were, in essence, invisible in the eyes of society.

The conditions in many orphanages were far from ideal, and it's disheartening to acknowledge that this mistreatment continues in some places today. One glaring area where these injustices are evident is in the necessities of life. Many orphanages struggled to provide proper nutrition for the children under their care. A balanced diet, essential for healthy growth and development, is often a luxury these children can't afford. The lack of access to clean water compounded their suffering, leading to health issues that could have been easily prevented.

Furthermore, the limited space available for these children to play and explore hindered their physical and emotional development. Play is not just about fun; it's a fundamental part of childhood that fosters creativity, social skills, and a sense of belonging. These children are denied a crucial aspect of their development without adequate play areas.

The shortage of clothing added to their plight. Children grow rapidly, and without a steady supply of clothes that fit, they are forced to deal with whatever is available. This not only affected their comfort but also their self-esteem and confidence.

Another area where these children had no control was in matters of faith. Their right to choose their religion or belief system is often denied. In some instances, religious institutions imposed their faith on these children, robbing them of the autonomy to make their own spiritual choices.

In remote areas, the loss of cultural identity is a heartbreaking consequence of this neglect. These children often found themselves cut off from their cultural heritage, unable to connect with their roots and traditions. The loss of culture isn't just a loss for the individual; it's a loss for society as a whole, as diverse cultures enrich our world in immeasurable ways.

Nonetheless, the bright side is that change has been happening. Over time, the implementation of human rights has slowly but surely brought about significant improvements in the lives of these vulnerable children. These rights, which recognize every child's inherent dignity and worth, have acted as a shield, protecting countless children from harm.

One of the most significant changes has been a growing awareness of children's rights. As societies have become more informed about the importance of safeguarding children's rights, there has been a shift in attitudes and actions. Governments, NGOs, and concerned individuals have come together to address the issues that have plagued orphanages and vulnerable children for so long.

There is a significant shortfall in providing nutritious meals, clean water access, and suitable play and recreation spaces. These changes are needed to enhance the children's physical well-being and also their emotional and cognitive development.

The recognition of children's right to choose their religion or belief system must gain ground. Children must now be given the freedom to explore their spirituality in a way that aligns with their own beliefs rather than having faith imposed upon them.

In some developed areas, efforts have been made to preserve and celebrate cultural diversity. This includes providing opportunities for children to connect with their cultural roots, learn about their traditions, and celebrate their heritage.

While significant progress is slowly being made, much work remains to be done. The mistreatment of children, especially those in vulnerable situations like orphanages and refugee camps, persists in some parts of the world. We must continue to advocate for the rights and well-being of all children, ensuring they can grow, learn, and thrive in a safe and nurturing environment.

How we treat our children today shapes the leaders and citizens of tomorrow. The mistreatment and neglect of children, especially those in orphanages, refugee camps, and on the streets, have been a dark stain on our history. However, there is hope on the horizon. The implementation of human rights has paved the way for positive change, and while challenges remain, progress is being made to ensure that all children can reach their full potential and become the leaders our world needs. We must continue to work together to protect and uplift the most vulnerable among us, for their future is intertwined with the future of our society as a whole.

When discussing the topic of human rights, it is crucial to direct our attention towards the rights of children and, subsequently, examine how poverty constrains the opportunities for children and young people to realize their full potential. The Universal Declaration of Human Rights, established in 1948 and embraced by fifty-six member nations of the United Nations, marked a pivotal moment when children were recognized and acknowledged as individuals possessing inherent human rights. Since that significant moment, children have progressively inherited these universal human rights.

Human rights are fundamental needs and freedoms that are inherent to all individuals from the moment of their birth until the end of their lives. They are founded on fundamental principles such as equality, dignity, respect, and the innate freedom that comes with our existence. The United Nations, as a global body, insists that these rights should always prioritize the child's best interests. This implies that every effort should be made to ensure that children are placed at the center of attention so that they can fully benefit from these rights.

According to the United Nations, a child is defined as "any human under the age of 18 years old." However, it is disheartening to note that many of these children lead lives mired in poverty due to various circumstances, including the loss of parents, the ravages of war, drought, famine, and other adverse factors.

When addressing the issue of child poverty, we are essentially acknowledging that these young individuals lack the necessary support and resources required to meet their fundamental life needs. These essentials encompass basic requirements such as access to nourishing food, adequate clothing, and secure shelter. When children find themselves in the dire situation of not having enough to eat, wearing presentable clothes, or having access to clean water, the negative consequences far outweigh any positive aspects.

One of the most concerning repercussions is the adverse impact on their health, primarily caused by drinking contaminated water and inadequate sanitation facilities. Take, for instance, children and youths living in orphanages, on reserve lands, and in refugee camps who have no choice but to drink unsafe water. It is well-documented that unclean water can lead to severe health complications. Moreover, some of these children experience heightened stress and a sense of shame, as their lack of proper clothing prevents them from comfortably socializing with their peers in their communities.

Several groups of children and youths are particularly vulnerable to pervasive poverty. This includes those who live apart from their parents, children residing in orphanages, those growing up in single-parent households, and individuals born into impoverished families. It is imperative that we prioritize these children and youth, as they face unique and acute challenges stemming from their impoverished circumstances.

Efforts to address child poverty should encompass comprehensive strategies that provide immediate relief in terms of food, clothing, and shelter and address the root causes of poverty. These initiatives should aim to break the cycle of poverty and create opportunities for these young individuals to thrive and reach their full potential. By focusing on the most vulnerable among us, we can work towards a more equitable and just society where every child has the chance to lead a healthy and prosperous life.

How are They Being Harmed?

In certain communities, adolescents are often exploited to secure their basic sustenance. This distressing reality is particularly prevalent in numerous refugee settlements, where parents sometimes compel their young ones to undertake labour that exceeds their physical capacity in exchange for a small amount of meal.

Moreover, children naturally seek outlets for amusement and play to nurture their physical and cognitive development. When they muster the courage to approach their caregivers, beseeching for toys or entertainment, their pleas are rejected, and they are often confined to isolation. Regrettably, it is challenging for them to fathom that their parents or guardians are responsible for providing them with the tools and opportunities for play during their formative years.

This predicament is acutely pronounced among children living within orphanages or originating from such environments. For these youngsters, the struggle for survival extends beyond just securing food and shelter; they must contend with a dearth of emotional and psychological support. In many instances, their voices and rights are entirely disregarded and forsaken.

Society must recognize the profound hardships faced by these vulnerable children and adolescents. Efforts should be channelled towards meeting their immediate material needs and creating an environment where their emotional and developmental requirements are acknowledged and fulfilled. By doing so, we can aspire to foster a more compassionate and equitable society where every child's right to well-rounded development is safeguarded and upheld.

One significant aspect highlighting how poverty restricts young people from realizing their fundamental rights is when young individuals from immigrant backgrounds are compelled to work long hours to secure funds for their daily expenses and education. In this scenario, the cherished right to receive an education from their parents is often sidelined or abandoned.

Moreover, children with parents who have disabilities may experience a sense of alienation and diminished love, as they often find themselves in a position where they must assist their physically challenged parents with mobility tasks, such as moving or pushing them around. This circumstance often results in the erosion of their right to be nurtured and cared for in the typical parent-child dynamic. Essentially, the burdens of caregiving and economic necessity can overshadow the fundamental rights and well-being of these youths.

These situations underscore the pressing need to address poverty's far-reaching consequences, as it impacts the economic well-being of families and disrupts the fulfillment of essential rights, particularly those related to education, protection, and emotional well-being for young individuals from various backgrounds. It calls for a collective effort to provide support systems and opportunities that allow these youths to fully enjoy their rights and lead dignified lives despite the challenges posed by poverty and unique family circumstances.

Certainly, poverty is a formidable impediment to the development and progress of young adults. It casts a shadow over the lives of countless children and youths, thwarting their ability to realize their fundamental rights fully. As front-line workers, it is imperative that we intensify our efforts by conducting comprehensive workshops aimed at imparting a profound understanding of these rights to parents, guardians, and anyone entrusted with the upbringing of children. It is essential to acknowledge that children are, without question, human beings, and as such, they inherit inalienable human rights from the moment they come into this world. Consequently, any endeavour undertaken to promote and protect human rights must be carried out with the utmost consideration for the well-being of children.

In our collective pursuit to uphold the rights of young adults, it is vital to appreciate the intergenerational impact of our actions. By empowering today's youth with a firm understanding of their rights, we equip them with the knowledge and tools to advocate for these rights for themselves and future generations. This proactive approach ensures that the principles of justice, dignity, and equality continue to flourish, becoming an enduring legacy passed down to their own children and beyond.

At the heart of this endeavour is the recognition that poverty perpetuates a cycle of deprivation, often beginning in childhood and extending into adulthood. Young individuals growing up in impoverished households frequently find their opportunities and potential stifled by the harsh realities of economic hardship. The rights that should rightfully belong to them—rights to education, healthcare, protection, and participation—are all too often denied or curtailed due to financial constraints.

One of the most profound consequences of poverty on young adults is the limitation it places on their access to quality education. Education is not merely a privilege but a fundamental right that forms the bedrock of personal development and societal progress. Yet, impoverished families often struggle to provide their children with the educational opportunities they deserve. Many young individuals from low-income backgrounds are compelled to forego their educational pursuits to contribute financially to their family's meager resources. This vicious cycle perpetuates the intergenerational transmission of poverty, as the lack of education restricts future employment prospects and earning potential.

Again, poverty can also expose young adults to precarious living conditions, inadequate healthcare, and limited access to essential services. The right to adequate housing, safe living environments, and healthcare are integral components of human rights, but they often remain elusive for those trapped in poverty. Young adults grappling with financial hardship may find themselves living in substandard housing, lacking access to nutritious food, and struggling to access medical care when needed. These circumstances not only undermine their physical and mental well-being but also compromise their ability to reach their full potential.

Additionally, the right to protection is paramount for young adults, especially in the context of poverty. Economic hardship can make young individuals more vulnerable to exploitation, abuse, and involvement in illicit activities. They may be coerced into child labour or become victims of trafficking due to their desperate circumstances. The absence of a protective safety net exacerbates their vulnerability, depriving them of the safeguards necessary for a safe and secure upbringing.

To address these challenges and break the poverty cycle, it is imperative that we take a proactive and holistic approach. First and foremost, education must be at the forefront of our efforts. We must work tirelessly to ensure that all young individuals, regardless of their socioeconomic background, have access to quality education. This includes providing financial support to families in need and also creating an inclusive educational system that caters to diverse learning needs.

Furthermore, we must advocate for policies and programs that alleviate the economic burden on impoverished families. This could involve initiatives such as affordable housing, food assistance programs, and accessible healthcare services. By addressing the material needs of young adults and their families, we can mitigate the adverse effects of poverty and create a more equitable society.

In tandem with these efforts, it is essential to raise awareness about the rights of young adults. Workshops and educational campaigns, as mentioned earlier, play a pivotal role in ensuring that parents, guardians, and caregivers understand and respect these rights. When individuals are aware of the rights of young adults, they are more likely to make informed decisions that prioritize the well-being and development of the next generation.

Ultimately, our commitment to upholding the rights of young adults is an investment in the future. By empowering them with education, protection, and opportunities, we empower them to break free from the shackles of poverty and to become active, responsible citizens who can contribute positively to society. Moreover, we enable them to pass on the legacy of human rights to their own children, perpetuating a cycle of progress and dignity that transcends generations.

Indeed, poverty is indeed a formidable obstacle to the realization of fundamental rights for young adults. As front-line workers and advocates, we must redouble our efforts to raise awareness about these rights, alleviate the economic burdens impoverished families face, and provide access to quality education and essential services. By doing so, we empower young individuals to thrive and ensure that the principles of justice, equality, and dignity endure as a legacy for generations to come. The path to progress begins with recognizing that children are not only the bearers of human rights but also the torchbearers of a brighter future.

CHAPTER III

LIFE IN CONGO DRC

The Democratic Republic of Congo (DRC) stands as a formidable presence in Sub-Saharan Africa, being the largest country in terms of size and the second largest on the entire African continent. With its expansive territory and population surpassing 84 million in 2018, the DRC holds significant potential for economic prosperity and social development. This vast nation is renowned for its natural wealth, including an array of valuable minerals such as diamonds, gold, copper, cobalt, and natural gas, among many others. These abundant resources have bestowed upon the DRC the title of the richest country in Africa. However, despite this wealth, the majority of the Congolese people have yet to reap the benefits of their nation's natural endowments.

The Democratic Republic of Congo is a veritable treasure trove of minerals and natural resources. Its vast deposits of diamonds, renowned for their quality, have earned the country its nickname as the "Diamond Capital of the World." Alongside diamonds, the DRC boasts extensive reserves of gold, copper, cobalt, and natural gas, among other minerals. These resources have immense economic value and are highly sought after in the global market. In fact, the DRC's mineral wealth has played a significant role in shaping international trade and economic dynamics.

Cobalt is a mineral of immense importance in the modern world. It is a key component in lithium-ion batteries, which power a wide range of electronic devices, from smartphones to electric vehicles. The DRC is the world's largest producer of cobalt, accounting for more than 60% of global production. It positions the country at the center of the electric vehicle revolution and the growing demand for renewable energy sources.

Historical Context: A Legacy of Exploitation

The story of the Democratic Republic of Congo's mineral wealth is intertwined with a complex history of exploitation, conflict, and foreign interference. The nation's modern history can be traced back to the late 19th century when it was colonized by King Leopold II of Belgium. Under his brutal rule, the Congolese people endured forced labour, widespread violence, and the extraction of resources to enrich the Belgian monarchy.

After gaining independence from Belgium in 1960, the DRC faced a tumultuous period marked by political instability, coups, and civil wars. These conflicts were partly fueled by the scramble for the country's valuable resources. Various rebel groups and neighbouring countries became involved in the conflict, further exacerbating the situation. The wealth generated from resource extraction often funded armed groups, perpetuating violence and instability.

In 1997, Laurent-Désiré Kabila came to power, promising a new era of stability and prosperity for the DRC. However, his reign was marked by corruption, authoritarianism, and ongoing conflict. The DRC's mineral wealth continued to be a source of both economic potential and conflict.

Challenges to Development

While the Democratic Republic of Congo possesses immense mineral wealth, it has struggled to translate these resources into tangible benefits for its people. Several key challenges have impeded the country's development and hindered the equitable distribution of wealth.

Corruption: Corruption has been a persistent issue in the DRC. Government officials and elites have often siphoned off wealth from resource extraction, diverting it away from public coffers and into private pockets. This corruption has resulted in a lack of funds for critical infrastructure, healthcare, education, and other essential services.

Infrastructure Deficits: The DRC's vast size and challenging terrain make the development of infrastructure, such as roads, railways, and electricity grids a formidable task. Insufficient infrastructure limits the ability to transport goods, access remote areas, and provide basic services to the population.

Political Instability: Political instability and dictatorship have created an uncertain business environment, deterring foreign investment and hindering economic growth. The lack of a stable governance structure has also made it difficult to implement long-term development plans.

Conflict and Security Concerns: Ongoing conflict in certain regions of the DRC disrupts economic activities and displaces communities. Armed groups continue to vie for control over mining areas, exacerbating insecurity and impeding the responsible extraction of resources.

Environmental Concerns: The extraction of minerals and natural resources in the DRC has often occurred without adequate environmental safeguards, leading to deforestation, water pollution, and other environmental issues. This not only harms ecosystems but also jeopardizes the livelihoods of local communities.

Efforts Towards Change

Despite these challenges, there have been positive developments aimed at harnessing the DRC's mineral wealth for the benefit of its people. International initiatives and advocacy groups have called for greater transparency in the mining sector, advocating for measures to combat corruption and promote responsible resource extraction.

The DRC itself has taken steps to address some of these issues. In 2019, the government initiated a review of mining contracts and imposed higher royalties on certain minerals. These measures were intended to ensure a fairer share of the profits from resource extraction would flow into the national treasury.

International organizations and NGOs have also supported efforts to improve governance, build infrastructure, and promote sustainable development in the DRC. These initiatives aim to address some of the root causes of the country's challenges and create a more equitable and stable future.

The Democratic Republic of Congo is a paradoxical example of immense natural wealth coexisting with persistent poverty and instability. Its vast mineral resources have the potential to transform the nation and improve the lives of its citizens. Conversely, historical exploitation, dictatorship, corruption, political instability, and ongoing conflict have hindered the realization of this potential.

Efforts to address these challenges are ongoing, with calls for greater transparency, responsible resource extraction, and improved governance. The DRC's journey towards harnessing its riches for the benefit of its people is fraught with complexities, but it is a journey that holds the promise of a brighter future. Ultimately, the fate of the Democratic Republic of Congo and its people will depend on overcoming these obstacles and creating a more equitable and prosperous nation.

Congo's Rich Natural Resources, Ongoing Conflict, and Personal Reflections

The Democratic Republic of Congo (DRC) has breathtaking natural beauty, abundant resources, and a complex history. While it is often celebrated for its vast wealth in minerals, it is also marred by ongoing conflicts and internal strife.

Congo's natural resources are among its most valuable assets. The country is blessed with a variety of minerals, including diamonds, gold, copper, cobalt, and more. These riches have earned Congo the reputation of being the wealthiest nation in Africa. Nonetheless, as with many resource-rich countries, the benefits of these bountiful reserves have not always trickled down to its people.

Diamonds have long been a symbol of luxury and opulence, and Congo's diamond deposits are particularly renowned for their quality and abundance. The allure of these precious gems, known as "blood diamonds," has, unfortunately, fueled conflict and exploitation in certain regions, where revenue from the diamond trade has funded armed groups and perpetuated violence.

Gold is another highly sought-after mineral in the DRC. Its beauty and rarity make it a valuable commodity in global markets. On the other hand, copper is a crucial component in various industries, including electronics and construction. Cobalt, an essential element in rechargeable batteries, places the DRC at the forefront of the green energy revolution.

Conflict and the Struggle for Control

A history of conflict and foreign intervention marks the story of the Democratic Republic of Congo. These conflicts have often been fueled by the desire to control the country's valuable resources. The legacy of colonialism, with Belgium as the colonial power, left a deep scar on the nation. The exploitation and brutality experienced during this period laid the groundwork for a fractured and unstable post-independence era.

My Education in Congo

Before delving into the broader issues facing Congo, let me share a glimpse of my personal experiences with education in the country. Education is critical to any society, and Congo is no exception. A mix of challenges and opportunities marked my time in Congolese schools.

Access to quality education in Congo is not evenly distributed. While there are schools in urban areas that provide relatively good education, many rural regions need more educational infrastructure. Class sizes can be large, resources scarce, and teachers may not always receive the support and training they need.

Despite these challenges, the students have a thirst for knowledge. One of the remarkable aspects of education in Congo is the determination and resilience of the students and teachers. Despite limited resources, students are eager to learn and make the most of their educational opportunities. Often underpaid and overworked, teachers do their best to impart knowledge and inspire their students. The passion for learning is palpable and serves as an evidence to the resilience of the Congolese people.

Conflict and the Challenges of Daily Life

Returning to the broader picture, the conflict in Congo has had far-reaching consequences for the daily lives of its people. The country has faced a series of wars and internal conflicts that have displaced millions and left communities in turmoil. In some regions, armed groups continue to vie for control over mining areas, perpetuating insecurity and hindering responsible resource extraction.

The impact of these conflicts extends beyond displacement and insecurity. It has eroded trust in government institutions, disrupted essential services, and perpetuated poverty. The wealth generated from resource extraction has often been misappropriated, deepening the divide between the ruling elites and the general population.

Inequality and the Struggle for Prosperity

Congo's rich natural resources have not translated into widespread prosperity. Inequality remains a stark reality, with a significant portion of the population living in poverty. The concentration of wealth in the hands of a few exacerbates social tensions and undermines the country's potential for sustainable development.

Corruption is a persistent issue that hampers progress. Funds that should be invested in healthcare, education, and infrastructure are often siphoned off by corrupt officials. This leaves essential services underfunded and inaccessible to many Congolese.

Hope and Resilience

Amid the challenges, there is hope. The Congolese people are resilient and resourceful. They have weathered decades of turmoil and have shown an unwavering commitment to building a better future. Civil society organizations, local leaders, and international partners work together to address the root causes of conflict, promote good governance, and ensure responsible resource management.

The Democratic Republic of Congo is a land of paradoxes, where the beauty of its natural resources contrasts sharply with the challenges of ongoing conflict, inequality, and corruption. My personal experiences in Congolese schools underscore the determination of the people to overcome adversity through education. While the road ahead is fraught with obstacles, there is hope that concerted efforts and a commitment to justice and transparency can pave the way for a brighter future for Congo and its people.

Early Education and Life Challenges in the Democratic Republic of Congo

My journey through early education in the Democratic Republic of Congo (DRC) began in the village of Tchankombo, where I attended kindergarten. This experience was my first taste of formal education in a country where challenges and uncertainties often accompanied the pursuit of learning. I will recount my personal experiences and explore the broader educational landscape in the DRC, shedding light on the impact of historical events and conflicts on access to education.

Kindergarten Education in Tchankombo, My Beautiful Small Village

My educational journey in the DRC commenced in the village of Tchankombo, where kindergarten served as my first formal introduction to learning. The curriculum encompassed various subjects, and instruction was primarily conducted in French, one of the country's official languages. Tchankombo's kindergarten was the sole educational institution in our village, making it a central hub for early learning.

The limited resources in our village meant that our school had only three classes. Consequently, when a student completed the third class, they had to wait until new classes were constructed to begin the next academic year, typically starting with grade one. This practice highlighted the challenges of providing continuous education in rural areas of the DRC, where infrastructure development lagged behind educational needs.

Interruption of Education Due to Conflict

However, my educational journey was abruptly interrupted, and my progression to grade one was delayed due to the consequences of conflict in the DRC. The Alliance of Democratic Forces for the Liberation of Congo (AFDL) launched an attack on the country, resulting in widespread turmoil and devastation. My village, Tchankombo, was severely affected by this conflict, leading to a series of life-altering events.

One evening stands out in my memory as a turning point. I was at school, my parents were working on our farm, and my elder brother accompanied them. On that fateful day, we were instructed to sleep on the extremely dusty floor of our school. As young children, discomfort and fear quickly overcame us, and tears started to flow. We cried to walk back home to the comfort and safety of our families. However, the teachers, understanding the precarious situation, did not allow us to leave the school premises. We remained in that dusty, dimly lit classroom, longing for our parents.

It took a considerable amount of time before my parents could finish their work on the farm and return to pick me up from school. The journey home was filled with uncertainty, as the conflict had disrupted daily life in our village. This harrowing experience left a lasting impression on me, illustrating how the spectre of conflict could disrupt not only education but also the sense of security and normalcy in the lives of children.

Challenges of Access to Education in the DRC

My personal experience is just one small window into the broader challenges faced by students and families in the DRC. The country's education system has long grappled with a myriad of difficulties, many of which are rooted in its turbulent history.

Infrastructure Deficits: As evidenced by the delayed construction of new classrooms in my village, the lack of adequate educational infrastructure is a pervasive issue in the DRC. Many schools in rural areas are underfunded and lack the basic facilities required for effective teaching and learning.

Security Concerns: Ongoing conflict and instability in certain regions of the DRC pose a significant threat to education. Schools are often targeted, and students and teachers alike face the risk of violence and displacement. This disrupts education and creates an environment of fear and uncertainty.

Access to Quality Education: While access to education is considered a fundamental right in the DRC, disparities persist. Rural areas often lack well-trained teachers, teaching materials, and access to technology. This results in an uneven educational landscape where urban students may have more opportunities than their rural counterparts.

Economic Challenges: Many families in the DRC struggle with poverty, making it difficult for them to cover the costs associated with education, such as uniforms and school supplies. Also, the need for children to contribute to household income can sometimes take precedence over their education.

Efforts for Change and Hope for the Future

Despite these challenges, there are efforts to improve the educational landscape in the DRC. Government initiatives, non-governmental organizations, and international partners are working together to address the infrastructure deficit, provide teacher training, and expand access to quality education. Advocacy for children's rights to education remains a crucial part of these efforts.

My personal experience of waiting for my parents in that dusty classroom shows the true hardship and resilience of children in the face of adversity. It highlights the determination to learn and the enduring hope for a better future. It also underscores the importance of education as a beacon of stability and opportunity in a country marked by turmoil.

My early education in the Democratic Republic of Congo was marked by both the promise of learning and the harsh realities of conflict and adversity. The challenges students and families face in the DRC reflect broader issues related to education, infrastructure, security, and economic hardships. However, there is hope for change, as efforts are underway to improve the educational landscape and provide a brighter future for the children of Congo.

Escaping Conflict: A Family's Journey from Fear to Hope

In times of war, some human spirit often finds the strength to overcome seemingly insurmountable challenges. One such story is that of a family who, against all odds, managed to escape a war-torn village where bullets rained down like a deadly hailstorm. In the following narrative, we will explore the harrowing experience of this family as they navigated through the chaos of war, ultimately making the heart-wrenching decision to leave their beloved village in search of safety and a brighter future.

The Start of the Nightmare:

Did the bullet stop us? This haunting question serves as a grim reminder of the terror that engulfed my family's life. The response, however, is a fact of the unwavering determination of a mother to protect her child. "No," she says, "my mum carried me on her back, and we went step by step till we reached home." In a world shattered by conflict, where fear gripped the hearts of all, the bond between a mother and her child provided the strength to endure.

As the war raged on, bullets became the deadly orchestra of daily life. The echoes of gunfire were the background score to a life lived in constant fear. It was a time when homes became sanctuaries, and families huddled together, praying for safety. The war stopped for a while, and people started coming out of their houses again because everyone was hiding inside their homes. This brief respite allowed a glimpse of hope to shine through the dark clouds of despair.

The Fateful Decision:

During this fragile pause in the violence, my family faced a decision that would shape our future. Rumours spread like wildfire through the village, and one in particular sent shivers down our spines: all men were to be taken by force and join the army. It was a horrifying prospect, one that no parent could bear to accept. So, amid uncertainty and danger, my parents made the agonizing choice to leave the village behind.

Our destination was Uvira, a place within the same country but far from the familiar comforts of our village. It was a journey into the unknown, driven by the desperate hope of escaping the clutches of a war that had torn our lives apart. With heavy hearts and little more than the clothes on our backs, we embarked on a perilous journey that would test our strength and resilience to the fullest.

The Perilous Journey:

Leaving the village was a heart-wrenching experience. We left behind not only our villager-looking homes but also our memories, neighbours, and the life we had known for generations. As we set out for Uvira, uncertainty hung over us like a dark cloud, and the road ahead was fraught with danger.

The journey was anything but easy. We navigated through treacherous terrain, traversing rugged landscapes and dense forests. Food was scarce, and water even scarcer. We relied on our wits and resourcefulness to survive, gathering whatever we could find. Every step was a test of endurance, every night a gamble with our safety.

The Threat of Separation:

The threat of forced conscription loomed over us like a shadow. It was a constant fear that gnawed at our souls, a fear that our family would be torn apart. As we journeyed deeper into the unknown, our bond grew stronger. Each parent held their children closer, and siblings clung to each other, finding hope in the shared struggle.

Despite the hardships and the ever-present danger, the family pressed on, fueled by the hope of finding safety in Uvira. It was a beacon of light on the horizon, a place where they could rebuild our shattered lives and protect our children from the horrors of war.

Arrival in Uvira:

After what seemed like an eternity, we finally arrived in Uvira. The journey had taken a toll on us, both physically and emotionally. We were weary, our clothes tattered, but our spirits remained unbroken. Uvira offered a glimmer of hope, a sanctuary from the war that had driven us 120 kilometres from our village.

Life in Uvira was far from perfect, but it was a respite from the constant threat of violence. The family settled into our new surroundings, grateful for the safety and relative stability we found. We worked hard to rebuild our lives, finding ways to make ends meet. It was a journey marked by hardship, danger, and uncertainty but also a journey filled with hope and resilience. In the face of adversity, this family's love for one another and our determination to survive carried us through the darkest of times.

Reflecting on my journey, I am inspired to appreciate the safety and security many of us often take for granted. May we also remember the countless families around the world who continue to face the horrors of conflict and displacement, and may we work towards a world where no one must make the agonizing choice to leave our homes in search of safety and a brighter future.

Life in Uvira, a small town in the eastern part of the Democratic Republic of Congo, had its share of tumultuous moments, but amidst the chaos, there was a glimmer of normalcy. For me, this semblance of normal life began to take shape in the early 2000s when I was sent back to school at the Kahelele Primary School.

It was 2001, and Uvira was still reeling from the effects of a long-standing conflict that had ravaged the region for years. Despite the challenges, the resumption of school brought a ray of hope to many young minds like mine. The Kahelele Primary School, my newfound academic sanctuary, would be the place where my educational journey resumed.

One significant aspect of our education in Uvira was the use of the French language. As said earlier, French is one of the official languages of the Democratic Republic of Congo, and it was the medium of instruction at Kahelele Primary School. This linguistic shift was a significant adjustment for me, as my previous exposure to formal education had primarily been in Swahili, one of the country's other official languages. However, I embraced the opportunity to learn and adapt to this new linguistic environment.

School days at Kahelele Primary School were intense, but they gave us structure and purpose. We had a wide array of subjects to tackle each day, ranging from mathematics and science to history and geography. The curriculum was rigorous, and the long hours we spent at school were a testimony to our commitment to education.

Our school week was demanding, stretching from Monday to Saturday. Each day, we would start our classes promptly at 7:30 am and continue until 12:30 pm. These hours were validation to our dedication and a reflection of the importance placed on education in our community. Despite the challenges and hardships that many families faced, parents and guardians understood the value of education as a pathway to a brighter future for their children.

I found solace and purpose within the walls of my school. I genuinely enjoyed being in class, eager to absorb knowledge like a sponge. My teachers played a vital role in fostering my enthusiasm for learning. Their dedication and passion for education were palpable, and they instilled in me a love for learning that has stayed with me throughout my life.

In addition to my fondness for learning, I had the privilege of being recognized as an intelligent student in my class. This recognition brought a sense of pride and accomplishment that fueled my desire to excel academically. It also reinforced the importance of hard work and determination in achieving one's goals.

My time at Kahelele Primary School was about more than just academics. It was a period of personal growth and development. I learned valuable life skills, such as discipline, time management, and working collaboratively with my peers. These skills would prove to be valuable as I navigated the challenges that lay ahead in my life.

Beyond the classroom, I also forged meaningful friendships with my fellow students. We shared dreams and aspirations, and we supported each other in our pursuit of education. These friendships transcended the classroom and became a source of strength and resilience as we faced the uncertainties of life in Uvira.

As I reflect on those formative years at Kahelele Primary School, I am grateful for the opportunities it provided me. Despite the adversity surrounding us, the school became a beacon of hope, a place where young minds could flourish and dreams could take root.

Life in Uvira was far from easy, but my experience at Kahelele Primary School offered a sense of normalcy and purpose. The use of the French language, the rigorous curriculum, and the long school days were all part of the journey towards a brighter future. I cherished my time at school, where I thrived academically and developed crucial life skills and lasting friendships—these early years of education in Uvira laid the foundation for my future endeavours, instilling in me a deep appreciation for the value of knowledge and the resilience to overcome adversity.

It was 2002, and the tranquil routine of life at Kahelele Primary School in Uvira was shattered abruptly by the distant yet unmistakable sound of bullets. The atmosphere in the school became tense as uncertainty gripped teachers and students. The question that loomed was whether to send the students home or keep them sheltered within the open classrooms, bracing for the unknown.

I was a third grader, still a child in many ways, unaware of the gravity of the situation unfolding around me. The innocence of a child shielded me from comprehending the imminent danger that lurked in the distant echoes of gunfire. In a strange twist of fate, my friends and I found ourselves chuckling at the eerie sound of bullets, oblivious to the potential calamity that lay ahead.

For the teachers, the situation was vastly different. Fear gnawed at them; their hearts were weighed down by the responsibility of protecting their young charges. The decision they had to make was a heart-wrenching one—whether to release us to our homes in haste or keep us within the relative safety of the school premises. It was a dilemma born of uncertainty, and they grappled with the best course of action.

With its deafening gunshots, the outbreak of war was a nightmarish spectre that had haunted Uvira before. Memories of past conflicts cast a long shadow, and the prospect of history repeating itself was a chilling thought. The bullets, once distant and almost surreal, grew louder and more menacing with each passing moment.

As the situation deteriorated, Uvira town seemed to close its doors as if barricading itself against the impending storm of violence. Panic swept through the streets, and a collective rush to return home ensued. Every parent and every guardian was gripped by the urgent need to reach their loved ones and shield them from the impending storm.

At this critical juncture, parents who owned cars raced to Kahelele Primary School, their vehicles providing a lifeline in this crisis.

The escalating conflict was not limited to the unsettling sound of bullets—the ominous rumble of bombs added to the terror that had gripped the town. People, innocent civilians, were falling victim to the violence, their lives tragically cut short on the very streets they called home. The once-familiar landscape of Uvira had transformed into a battlefield, a place where the line between safety and danger had blurred beyond recognition.

Amidst this chaos and fear, the teachers at Kahelele Primary School faced an agonizing decision. They recognized that the safety of the students and themselves was at stake. Leaving pupils in the classroom, where they would be vulnerable to the indiscriminate violence of war, was an unthinkable prospect. In a sombre and tearful moment, they made the gut-wrenching choice to let us go home.

With heavy hearts, our teachers sent us off, but they did so with fervent prayers that every student would reach their home safely. It was a desperate plea to a higher power, a hope that the young lives they had nurtured and cared for would remain unscathed in the face of this harrowing conflict.

The journey home was fraught with peril. The streets that had once felt safe were now treacherous, filled with uncertainty and fear. We clung to the fervent prayers of our teachers, hoping against hope that we would find our families intact and our homes secure.

During this chaos, the innocence that had shielded me from understanding the gravity of the situation began to erode. The sound of bullets, once a source of amusement, now echoed as a chilling reminder of the fragility of life in times of war. The events of that day would leave an indelible mark on my memory, a stark reminder of the horrors that conflict can bring.

The day the war resumed in Uvira in December 2002 was a day that forever altered the lives of the students and teachers at Kahelele Primary School. The initial laughter at the sound of bullets quickly gave way to the stark reality of impending danger. Teachers faced an agonizing decision but ultimately chose to release their students, driven by a desperate desire to ensure their safety. The streets of Uvira became a battlefield, and the journey home was fraught with peril. It was a day that shook our innocence and made us acutely aware of the harsh realities of life in a conflict-ridden region.

A Tale of Survival: A Day of Fear and Reunion

In the annals of our family history, there is a day that will forever be etched in our memories, a day marked by resilience, sacrifice, and an unwavering bond between siblings. It was a day that taught us the true meaning of love and survival. The day was like any other, yet it would be unlike any other we had experienced.

The sun had just begun its ascent into the sky, casting a warm golden hue over our small village. It was a day much like any other school day, filled with laughter, play, and the pursuit of knowledge. I was a young child then, and my elder brother was my protector and guide through the tumultuous childhood journey.

As the clock struck 3:00 pm, the bell rang, signalling the end of our school day. Little did we know that this ordinary day would soon take an extraordinary turn. We stepped out of the school gates, our hearts light with the promise of a carefree afternoon ahead. But fate had other plans.

A sudden eruption of chaos shattered the tranquillity of our village. Gunshots echoed through the air, sending shockwaves of fear rippling through the crowd. Panic ensued as people scrambled for cover, desperately seeking refuge from the impending danger. It was a scene straight out of a nightmare—one that no child should ever have to witness.

My legs grew heavy, and exhaustion began to overtake me. I could no longer run, and my brother, realizing the gravity of the situation, made a courageous decision. With tears streaming down his face, he hoisted me onto his back. His words, filled with both desperation and determination, still ring in my ears to this day. He said, "We are going to die together and at once. Come, I'll carry you so that if a bullet hits me in front, then it will hit you as well. If it hits your back, then I will die too." The depth of his love and sacrifice became painfully clear in that moment.

As we trudged through the chaos, my brother's arms supporting me, we held onto hope with all our might. We clung to the belief that we could defy the odds and make it home safely. We were just children, thrust into a world of violence and uncertainty, but our sibling bond gave us the strength to persevere.

Hours passed, each one feeling like an eternity, and the journey home seemed never-ending. We dodged bullets and witnessed the devastation around us, a stark reminder of the harsh realities of the world. By the grace of God, or perhaps Allah, we finally reached the familiar path leading to our humble abode. It was a moment of relief mixed with anxiety as we approached our home.

When we arrived, we were met with an unsettling sight. Our parents were not there to greet us. Fear gnawed at our hearts as we realized they had gone in search of their missing children. We were alone, hungry, and weary. Our empty stomachs ached, but we knew that food was a luxury we could not afford.

Our father arrived first, his presence bringing a glimmer of hope to our weary souls. I rushed to him, clinging to the lifeline of his embrace. My first question was about our mother, the beacon of love in our lives. "Is Mum safe, too? Where is she?"

In his reply, our father's voice carried a heavy burden of worry and uncertainty. He said, "We went to different locations because we couldn't know if you would come home with all these bullets flying around. I hope she is safe." The relief of seeing our father was bittersweet, as the uncertainty surrounding our mother's fate continued to cast a shadow over our joy.

Time seemed to stretch as we waited for any sign of our mother's return. An hour or so passed, and then we heard a voice—a voice filled with anguish and sorrow. It was the voice of a woman crying in the distance, and our hearts sank as we realized it could only be our mother.

As the voice drew nearer, its wails became more distinct, and our anxiety grew. We rushed outside, our hearts pounding, and there, through tear-filled eyes, we saw her. It was our beloved mother, her face stained with tears and her voice choked with grief. She had reached our school in search of her children, only to find a harrowing scene of devastation.

The tears streaming down her face mirrored the ones we had shed on our journey home. She cried because she had come face to face with the cruel hand of fate, witnessing many young pupils who had lost their lives that day. The most horrifying revelation was that even our school had been reduced to ashes, a grim testament to the violence that had swept through our town.

In her eyes, she had already mourned our loss, believing that we were among the casualties. She had prepared herself for the unbearable grief of losing her children, yet fate had other plans for us. She arrived home and found us alive and well despite the heavy bullets and the grim reports of casualties that had plagued that fateful day.

The reunion that followed was a mixture of tears, relief, and an overwhelming sense of gratitude. We clung to each other, a family reunited against all odds. The ordeal we had endured had strengthened our bonds, reminding us of the value of love, sacrifice, and the unbreakable ties that held us together as a family.

As the days turned into weeks and the scars of that traumatic day began to heal, we reflected on the profound lessons it had taught us. We learned that in the face of adversity, the love between siblings can be a source of unwavering strength. We realized that the kindness and resilience of our parents could see us through the darkest times.

That day, we also understood the fragility of life and the importance of cherishing every moment with our loved ones. It was a reminder that peace should never be taken for granted and that the horrors of war can shatter the innocence of childhood in an instant.

In the years that followed, our family carried the scars of that day with us, a constant reminder of the fragility of life. Yet, we also carried the enduring spirit of survival and the indomitable power of love and family bonds. We grew stronger together, determined to create a better future and to ensure that the sacrifices made on that fateful day would not be in vain.

Running Out of the Country

The Human Exodus: Fleeing the Perils of the Democratic Republic of Congo

The Democratic Republic of Congo, nestled in the heart of Africa, has witnessed decades of non-stop wars and instability for many years, rendering it one of the most perilous places to inhabit on the planet. This tumultuous period has driven countless Congolese to seek refuge in neighbouring countries like Tanzania, Zambia, Uganda, and Burundi. However, the journey to escape the horrors of their homeland was fraught with its own set of hardships. To reach safety across Lake Tanganyika, many embarked on treacherous boat journeys, facing the elements and the grim spectre of violence. This account delves into the harrowing experiences of those who left Congo in search of sanctuary, shedding light on the immense challenges they faced and the sacrifices made during their perilous exodus.

A Nation in Turmoil

The Democratic Republic of Congo has endured a tumultuous history marred by political instability, civil strife, and economic hardships. 1997 marked a turning point as a rebellion led by Laurent-Désiré Kabila toppled the long-time dictator Mobutu Sese Seko, bringing Kabila to power. This transition, however, did not usher in the promised era of stability and prosperity. Instead, the nation spiralled further into chaos, with a multitude of armed groups, both domestic and foreign, vying for control over its vast mineral wealth.

Faced with relentless violence, displacement, and a dire lack of basic necessities, many Congolese were left with no choice but to flee their homeland. For them, the journey to safety represented not only an escape from the horrors of conflict but also a quest for the possibility of a better life.

Seeking Refuge in Neighboring Nations

Neighbouring countries like Tanzania, Zambia, Uganda, and Burundi provided a glimmer of hope for those desperately seeking refuge from the violence and instability that engulfed the Democratic Republic of Congo. These countries, often sharing cultural, historical, and geographical ties with their Congolese neighbours, opened their borders and established refugee camps to accommodate the influx of people in dire need.

In this time of crisis, the strength of human resilience shone through as individuals and families embarked on arduous journeys, traversing vast distances on foot and seeking solace in foreign lands. Their arrival in these host countries marked the beginning of a new chapter in their lives, albeit one filled with uncertainty and challenges.

The Perilous Exodus

Leaving behind the chaos and danger of their homeland was a Herculean task. The journey to safety often involved traversing treacherous terrain, navigating through dense forests, and evading hostile forces that lurked along the way. Many families were separated, with loved ones lost or displaced during the arduous trek to the borders of neighbouring nations.

One of the most formidable obstacles on the path to safety was the daunting expanse of Lake Tanganyika. To cross this vast body of water, people had no choice but to rely on boats. However, the available boats were grossly inadequate to transport the thousands of desperate souls yearning to escape the horrors of Congo.

The Desperate Voyage Across Lake Tanganyika

Lake Tanganyika, the second deepest lake in the world, presented a formidable barrier to those seeking refuge. In their desperation, refugees and internally displaced individuals crowded onto small, rickety boats, hoping to reach the safety of foreign shores. These makeshift vessels were ill-equipped for the perilous journey that lay ahead.

The overcrowded boats teetered precariously on the edge of disaster as passengers clung to the hope of a better life across the lake. Tragically, many never reached their destination. The perilous voyage claimed the lives of countless individuals as boats capsized, sank, or succumbed to the unpredictable whims of the lake's tumultuous waters. The silent depths of Lake Tanganyika became a watery grave for those who had already endured so much suffering.

A Grim Fate at the Hands of Soldiers

While the natural perils of Lake Tanganyika were formidable, the threat of violence and hostility was equally ominous. The journey across the lake exposed refugees to a different kind of danger—the presence of armed soldiers and hostile groups. For many, the struggle for survival continued even as they attempted to flee their war-torn homeland.

Soldiers patrolling the shores of Lake Tanganyika subjected fleeing refugees to extortion, violence, and, in some cases, even death. The stories of those who escaped this fate were harrowing, filled with accounts of brutality and intimidation at the hands of those sworn to protect. This perilous journey across the lake, meant to be a pathway to safety, often turned into a nightmare of unimaginable proportions.

The Price of Freedom

The quest for freedom and safety came at an unimaginable cost for the refugees of the Democratic Republic of Congo. The exodus across Lake Tanganyika reflected their unshakeable resolve to escape the horrors of war, conflict, and instability. However, the toll on human lives, families, and communities was immense.

For many, the sacrifices made during this perilous journey were deeply personal and painful. The loss of loved ones, the trauma endured, and the uncertainty of life in a foreign land weighed heavily on those who survived. The refugee camps in neighbouring countries, though a sanctuary of sorts, were also a stark reminder of the displacement and upheaval that had torn their lives apart.

The Democratic Republic of Congo's turbulent history since 1997 has transformed it into one of the world's most dangerous and unstable regions. Lake Tanganyika, a seemingly insurmountable obstacle, became both a symbol of hope and a source of despair as desperate refugees braved treacherous waters, overcrowded boats, and the threat of violence to reach safety.

The stories of those who endured this harrowing exodus serve as a proof to the resilience of people and the indomitable will to survive. However, they also underscore the immense sacrifices made, the lives lost, and the trauma endured during their quest for freedom. The journey across Lake Tanganyika was a perilous path to salvation, forever changing the lives of those who embarked on it, leaving scars both visible and hidden as a true story of their unwavering determination to escape the horrors of war.

Throughout human history, countless families have embarked on journeys filled with uncertainty and fear, driven by the unrelenting pursuit of safety and a better life. Like so many others, our family found ourselves thrust into a perilous situation, compelled to leave behind our homeland and seek refuge in a foreign land. The catalyst for our journey was a family ticket, a fragile lifeline that transported us from the brink of despair to the shores of hope. This is the story of our journey, a journey that began with a family ticket and led us to Zambia, where we would commence our refugee life journey.

The world we knew was crumbling around us, torn apart by conflict, violence, and political unrest. It was a time when the very ground beneath our feet seemed to tremble with fear, and the air was thick with uncertainty. Our homeland, once a place of joy and belonging, had become a battleground where survival was a daily struggle. Amid this chaos, my father, a pillar of strength and determination, made a fateful decision: he purchased a family ticket.

This family ticket was more than just a piece of paper; it was our ticket to survival. It represented the hope that we could escape violence and find sanctuary in a distant land. With this precious ticket in hand, we boarded a boat, leaving behind everything we had ever known. It was a heart-wrenching departure, filled with tearful goodbyes and lingering memories of the life we were leaving behind.

As the boat set sail, we were filled with a mix of emotions. Fear gnawed at our hearts, but so did a glimmer of hope. We held on to the belief that there was a better life waiting for us, that somewhere beyond the horizon, we could rebuild what had been shattered. Our journey had begun.

The boat journey itself was arduous and filled with challenges. Crowded conditions, limited provisions, and the constant fear of being intercepted by hostile forces were our constant companions. But we clung to that family ticket, a symbol of our collective resilience and determination. It was a stark reminder that we were in this together as a family, and we could overcome any obstacle.

Finally, after what felt like an eternity, we arrived in Zambia. The moment our feet touched Zambian soil, a profound sense of relief washed over us. We had made it to safety. The promise of a new beginning had replaced the uncertainty of our journey.

With its welcoming spirit and open arms, Zambia offered us a haven. We were greeted by compassionate individuals and organizations dedicated to assisting refugees like us. It was here that our refugee life journey truly began. We faced the daunting task of building a new life from scratch, but we were not alone in this endeavour. The kindness and support of the Zambian people and the assistance of various humanitarian agencies provided us with the foundation we needed to start anew.

Life as a refugee was not without its challenges. We lived in makeshift shelters, relying on aid for our basic needs. The adjustment to a new culture and way of life was, at times, overwhelming, and the memories of our homeland often weighed heavily on our hearts. However, the indomitable spirit of our family and the resilience we had cultivated throughout our journey allowed us to persevere.

Education was a priority for our family, and we were grateful for the educational opportunities that Zambia provided for refugee children. Despite the challenging circumstances, we pursued our studies with determination, knowing that education was our pathway to a brighter future. The classrooms became a place of hope and aspiration, a place where we could envision a life beyond the confines of a refugee camp.

As the years passed, our family adapted to our new life in Zambia. We found work, formed friendships, and became part of a supportive community of fellow refugees. While our journey had been born out of desperation, it had also been a journey of resilience and strength. We had learned to lean on each other, to find joy in the simplest of moments, and to never lose sight of our dreams for a better future.

In time, Zambia became not just a place of refuge but a place we could call home. The bonds we formed with the people of Zambia remains unforgettable. We had come to appreciate the beauty of a country offering us sanctuary and a chance for a new beginning.

Our family's story is not unique; it is a story shared by countless refugees around the world. It is a story of courage in the face of adversity, of resilience in the wake of despair, and of hope that can transcend even the darkest of times. Our family ticket had been our lifeline, but our unwavering spirit had carried us through.

As I reflect on our journey, I am reminded of the strength that can be found in the bonds of family, the kindness of strangers, and the power of hope. Our journey was a fact to the human spirit's capacity to endure, to adapt, and to find solace in the most unexpected of places.

Today, we have rebuilt our lives in Zambia, while the scars of our past remain, they remind us of our journey. Our family ticket may have been the catalyst for our journey, but our unwavering determination propelled us forward. In Zambia, we found not only refuge but also a new beginning; for that, we are forever grateful.

Our journey began with a family ticket and led us to Zambia, on a refugee life journey that was marked by challenges but ultimately defined by resilience, hope, and the belief that a better tomorrow is always within reach.

CHAPTER IV

THE REASON WE BECAME REFUGEES

The Perils of Becoming a Refugee: Escaping War-Torn Congo DRC

In the modern world, the refugee crisis has reached unprecedented levels. According to the United Nations, a refugee is defined as "a person who is outside his or her country of nationality or habitual residence and has a well-founded fear of being persecuted because of their race, religion, or nationality." There are myriad reasons why individuals are compelled to become refugees, and among these reasons is the devastating impact of armed conflict. Let's explore the harrowing personal experience of one individual who was forced to leave their homeland, the Democratic Republic of Congo (DRC), due to the outbreak of war. The story not only sheds light on the horrors of war but also shows the truly dire circumstances that drive people to seek refuge in foreign lands.

The Descent into Chaos

The Democratic Republic of Congo, a country located in the heart of Africa, is no stranger to turmoil and conflict. A series of brutal wars, internal strife, and political instability mar its history. The protagonist of our narrative was living in this tumultuous environment when the eruption of war shattered their life. The onset of conflict in Congo DRC exposed countless civilians, including our narrator, to unimaginable horrors.

Direct Exposure to War

Amid the chaos, the protagonists of our story found themselves directly exposed to the brutalities of war. They recount the haunting memories of witnessing and hearing about people being mercilessly chopped to death. These gruesome scenes left indelible scars on their psyche, traumatizing them in ways that are difficult to comprehend for those who have not experienced such horrors firsthand. The trauma they endured was not just a momentary shock; it was a psychological burden that they would carry with them throughout their journey as a refugee.

The Loss of Hope

As the war raged on, hope began to evaporate. Like so many others in their situation, the protagonist started to question life's very essence. In a war-torn region, the line between life and death became dangerously blurred. The idea that men were supposed to die for no reason if they refused to join the military began to take hold. The harrowing reality was that refusing to enlist could lead to a senseless and gruesome demise. The prospect of a future without violence and fear seemed increasingly elusive.

The Youth Sacrificed

Among the most tragic aspects of war is the recruitment of young adults who are thrust into the conflict, often against their will. In the case of our narrator, they witnessed young people being compelled to join the ranks of warring factions. These young recruits, ill-prepared for the horrors of war, faced the very real possibility of losing their lives on the battlefield. The Alliance of Democratic Forces for the Liberation of Congo (AFDL), a notorious armed group operating in the region, was notorious for recruiting individuals as young as fourteen years old. These children were robbed of their innocence and thrust into a brutal world they could hardly comprehend.

The protagonist's story is just one of millions in a world where the refugee crisis continues to escalate. According to the United Nations High Commissioner for Refugees (UNHCR), the number of forcibly displaced people worldwide reached a staggering 82.4 million by the end of 2020. This includes refugees, asylum-seekers, and internally displaced persons, all of whom have been uprooted from their homes due to conflict, persecution, or violence.

The plight of refugees is a global humanitarian crisis that demands attention and action. It is a crisis that transcends borders and affects countries and communities worldwide. The responsibility to provide refuge and support to those fleeing conflict and persecution rests not only on the shoulders of host nations but also on the international community.

The Psychological Toll

Beyond the physical hardships and dangers faced by refugees, there is also a profound psychological toll. The trauma experienced by individuals who have witnessed and endured the horrors of war can be overwhelming. The scars left on the mind are often invisible but no less debilitating. Post-traumatic stress disorder (PTSD), anxiety, and depression are common among refugees who have experienced violence and displacement. These psychological wounds can persist long after physical safety has been attained, making the process of rebuilding one's life even more challenging.

The Quest for a Better Future

Refugees are driven by a powerful desire for a better future despite the immense challenges they face. They are resilient individuals who have demonstrated extraordinary strength in adversity. Like countless others, the protagonist of our story embarked on their journey as a refugee with the hope of finding safety, stability, and the opportunity to rebuild their life.

The global refugee crisis is a complex issue requiring concerted efforts from nations, organizations, and individuals. It is a crisis that calls upon the international community to uphold the principles of compassion, solidarity, and human rights. Providing refuge to those in need is not only a moral imperative but extending kindness to our shared humanity values.

As we reflect on the experiences of refugees like our protagonist, let us remember that behind every statistic is a human being with a story, a dream, and a longing for peace. It is our collective responsibility to extend a helping hand and create a world where no one is forced to become a refugee, where the horrors of war are replaced with the promise of hope and the possibility of a better future.

A Mother's Valor: Sheltering Her Family in the Midst of Disturbance

I remember my father, my elder brother, and I hiding under the bed. It was a memory etched into the deepest recesses of my mind, a memory that would forever resonate with the indomitable strength of a mother's love. The room was dimly lit, casting eerie shadows on the floor, and the air was thick with tension. The oppressive weight of uncertainty hung in the air as we cowered beneath the sturdy wooden bed frame.

In those tumultuous times, our homeland was gripped by conflict, a relentless storm that swept away the peace and security we once knew. Soldiers, clad in uniforms that symbolized authority and fear, roamed the streets with an insatiable thirst for young men to conscript into the ever-escalating conflict. It was an atmosphere of dread and despair where no one was truly safe.

My mother, with her unwavering courage and maternal instinct, was our guardian angel amidst this chaos. She would rise to the occasion, time and again, answering the door whenever the soldiers came knocking. Her response was our lifeline, the thread that held our fragile world together. "Yes, I have three strong boys, and they have been taken by previous soldiers," she would assert with a steady voice, her words a testament to her valour and quick thinking.

As the soldiers stood on our doorstep, their cold gazes scanning the room, my heart raced in my chest. My father, a once-proud man, now huddled beside us, his eyes a mirror of the fear and desperation that had gripped us all. My elder brother, usually a pillar of strength, clung to us, his grip trembling. We were a family driven to the brink, bound together by our shared vulnerability.

Though simple in structure, my mother's words carried the weight of our salvation. With each utterance, she spun a web of deception, a tapestry of lies that shielded us from the clutches of the soldiers. Her conviction was unwavering, her determination to protect her family unyielding. She knew that if the soldiers discovered us, they would not hesitate to tear us apart, consigning my father and brother to a grim fate on the frontlines.

The soldiers, fooled by her convincing façade, would eventually leave, their footsteps growing fainter as they moved on to the next house. And in those fleeting moments of reprieve, we would exhale the breath we didn't realize we were holding. My mother's ingenuity was a true love and length a mother would go to shield her children from the horrors of war.

Under the bed, we huddled together, the dust and darkness offering an unlikely sanctuary. Our family bond grew stronger in those cramped quarters, and our appreciation for our mother's heroism deepened. Her sacrifices were countless, her nights sleepless, and her heart heavy with the knowledge that she bore the burden of protecting us from a world gone mad.

As days turned into weeks and weeks into months, the conflict raged on, an unrelenting storm that refused to abate. The world outside remained unforgiving, and my mother continued to play her part in our clandestine charade. Each time the soldiers knocked, she would summon her inner strength, pushing aside her fears and worries to keep us safe.

But as the war dragged on, the toll on our family became increasingly evident. My father's health deteriorated, the constant fear and anxiety gnawing away at him. Once full of dreams and aspirations, my elder brother grew weary and despondent. And I, the youngest and most impressionable, clung to my mother's side, haunted by the spectre of the outside world.

One fateful day, as the sun cast long shadows across our besieged town, the soldiers arrived once more. But this time, they were different. They had heard rumours of my mother's subterfuge, and they were determined to uncover the truth. Their questions were sharper, their suspicion more palpable.

My mother, faced with their unyielding scrutiny, felt the weight of the world on her shoulders. She knew that her ruse was unravelling and that her family's safety hung in the balance. With tears in her eyes and a voice that quivered ever so slightly, she repeated her familiar refrain, 'Yes, I have three strong boys, and they have been taken by previous soldiers.'

We emerged from our hiding place, our hearts heavy but our spirits intact. My mother, her face pale and drawn, collapsed into a chair, the weight of the world finally lifted from her shoulders. In that moment, we understood the depth of her sacrifice and the lengths she had gone to protect her family from the horrors of war. We thought soldiers had stopped coming to rob our home; different groups of soldiers arrived and were quite determined. Even though my mom had explained that her two sons, my brother and I, were not around, they didn't listen and insisted on coming inside to check for themselves. Sadly, they ended up finding us under the bed.

They dragged my father up and began arguing with him. Things escalated quickly, and they started physically hurting him. It was a terrifying moment for our family, and we couldn't help but scream out of fear. Unfortunately, our cries only seemed to anger them more, and they turned their violence towards us all.

Both mom and dad suffered severe beatings that day. It was the first time I had ever witnessed my parents in tears, and it left a lasting mark on my young mind.

In the Democratic Republic of Congo (DRC), my family and I endured a horrifying and inexplicable ordeal. It all began when my brother was struck with the handle of a gun someday; they were in our house to rob. This brutal incident left us all in shock and fear, uncertain of what might happen next.

The violence we experienced was a grim reminder of the instability and danger that often plague the DRC. The region has a history of conflict and insecurity, with various armed groups vying for control and resources. This instability creates an environment where violence can erupt suddenly and without warning.

I felt like I was merely waiting for my own demise after my brother's assault. The pervasive sense of danger hung over us like a dark cloud, and we constantly feared for our lives. Every day was a struggle to survive, and the uncertainty of the future weighed heavily on our minds.

Our experience was unexplainable because it defied logic and reason. In a world that should prioritize peace and security, we found ourselves trapped in a nightmare where violence and brutality were commonplace. It was a stark reminder of the need for peace, stability, and the protection of human rights in places like the DRC.

Throughout this ordeal, my family and I clung to each other for support and strength. We hoped for a better future and dreamed of a day when we could live without the constant fear of violence.

With wounds and pain, my father made the brave decision to join a group of refugees who were fleeing the horrors of our homeland. We embarked on a perilous journey, setting our sights on the distant destination of Mpulungu, Zambia. Our means of escape? A rickety boat that would carry us across the vast and unforgiving Lake Tanganyika.

For two gruelling days, we clung to the hope of a safer future as the boat rocked and swayed on the turbulent waters. The lake, though beautiful, became a symbol of our uncertainty, its depths hiding both our fears and our dreams.

Finally, after what felt like an eternity, the boat docked in Mpulungu, Zambia. We had arrived at the border, but it was far from the end of our journey. At the border crossing, our family faced dire circumstances. We had no food to nourish our weary bodies, no clothes to shield us from the elements, and no peaceful place to rest our tired souls. All we possessed was an unbreakable spirit and a flicker of hope.

Despite our hardships, we clung to the belief that one day, we would find safety and peace. We longed for a future where the sound of people being killed and the terrifying echoes of bullets and bombs would be distant memories. Our journey was marked by suffering, but it was also defined by the resilience of the human spirit and the unwavering determination to build a better life far from the horrors of our past.

CHAPTER V

REFUGEE JOURNEY

How It Started

At a tender age, my heart was filled with many aspirations and ambitions that stretched before me like a vast, boundless horizon. I dreamed of becoming a doctor, lawyer, or engineer, and I imagined myself achieving greatness in my chosen field. My passion for education was fueled by a deep desire to learn and make a difference in the world. I envisioned myself securing a dignified profession, one that would allow me to contribute to society and make a positive impact on the lives of others.

However, the course of my life was altered by a catastrophic event that would change the trajectory of my journey. In 2003, my homeland was ravaged by war, unleashing an unrelenting tempest of chaos and destruction that shattered the very foundations of our existence. The war brought with it immense suffering and loss as families were torn apart, homes were destroyed, and lives were forever changed.

Faced with the harrowing reality of imminent danger and the crumbling infrastructure of my beloved homeland, I reluctantly bid farewell to the place I had always known as home. The poignant farewell to my birthplace was a sombre prelude to a perilous journey into the unknown.

As I crossed the border into Zambia, I left behind the ruins of my homeland and the dreams and aspirations that had once been the guiding stars of my life. The pursuit of education, the prospect of a respectable profession, and the hope of finding love and starting a family were all eclipsed by the pressing need for survival in a foreign land, far removed from the comforts and familiarity of home.

In the face of adversity, I was forced to adapt, to build a new life from the fragments of the old, and to find strength in the resilience of the human spirit. The war may have robbed me of my cherished dreams, but it could not diminish my determination to persevere, to carve out a future in a land that was both unfamiliar and challenging.

Despite the challenges ahead, I refused to give up on my dreams. I worked hard to adapt to my new surroundings, learning a new language, and embracing a new culture. I pursued education with new vigor, determined to excel in my studies and make a positive contribution to society. I found new friends and made connections that would help me to build a new life in Zambia.

Looking back on my journey, I realize that life has a way of steering us down unforeseen paths, testing our resolve, and shaping us into the individuals we become. While the dreams of my youth may have been deferred, the lessons learned and the experiences gained on this unexpected journey have endowed me with wisdom and resilience that I could never have anticipated.

And so, even though the dreams of a young heart were cast aside in the wake of conflict, I find solace in the knowledge that the indomitable spirit within me continues to endure, forging ahead with strong determination and seeking new dreams to embrace the ever-unfolding narrative of my life.

Start from M'pulungu to Mporokoso

The journey from Mpulungu in Zambia to Mporokoso in Kasama is a fascinating adventure that takes you through the heart of this beautiful African country. This journey is full of surprises and experiences that showcase Zambia's rich natural beauty, diverse culture, and local life.

Starting from Mpulungu, a picturesque town located on the shores of Lake Tanganyika in the northernmost part of Zambia, and dive into exploration of the Northern Province of Zambia. The road winds through rolling hills and forests, providing plenty of opportunities to appreciate Zambia's diverse flora and fauna. You'll be able to spot various animals, such as baboons, monkeys, and antelopes, on your way.

As you travel south, you'll encounter small towns and villages, such as Mbala or Isoka, where you can experience the warm hospitality and culture of the local people. You can indulge in traditional Zambian cuisine like *nshima*, a local delicacy made from maize meal, and interact with the friendly locals to learn about their customs and traditions.

Your journey will eventually take you to Kasama, the provincial capital of Northern Province. This lively town, with a mix of modern amenities and a strong sense of tradition, is a perfect place to explore local markets, visit historical sites, and engage with the local community to gain a deeper understanding of Zambian culture. Don't forget to visit the Chishimba Falls, a beautiful waterfall located just outside Kasama.

From Kasama, your journey to Mporokoso will take you deeper into the heart of the province. As you venture further into the countryside, the landscape becomes more rugged, with fewer towns and villages. This region is home to several game reserves, including the Mweru Wantipa National Park, where you can spot various wildlife, such as elephants, lions, and leopards.

As you approach Mporokoso, you'll notice the landscape changing once again, with rolling hills and fertile plains surrounding you. Mporokoso is a charming town amidst the Kasama region's natural beauty. It offers a tranquil atmosphere and a chance to unwind in a peaceful setting. The town's welcoming community, lush surroundings, and the opportunity to explore local traditions make it a delightful destination. Don't forget to visit the Mporokoso Museum to learn about the history and culture of the Bemba people, who are the dominant ethnic group in the region.

The journey from Mpulungu to Mporokoso in Zambia is a fascinating adventure that allows you to immerse yourself in the country's natural beauty, culture, and local life. Whether you're a nature enthusiast, a cultural explorer, or simply seeking a memorable journey, this route has something special to offer.

A Journey of Hope: Seven Years in M'porokoso Camp, Zambia

The term "refugee" evokes images of people forced to leave their homes and families due to conflict, persecution, or natural disasters. In the early 2000s, my family and I became refugees ourselves, fleeing from the war and persecution in our homeland. A perilous journey took us to Zambia's Northern Province, where we found refuge in the M'porokoso camp.

Our journey was not a smooth one. We had to leave behind everything we had ever known and embark on an uncertain path. We travelled for days, crossing borders and treacherous terrain, encountering other refugees with their own stories of loss and survival. We took each step with the weight of uncertainty, knowing we might never return home.

But we also found hope and resilience along the way. We formed bonds with strangers who became our companions on this arduous pilgrimage. We shared stories of our past and our dreams of a more peaceful future. We found strength in unity and resilience in the face of adversity.

When we arrived at the M'porokoso camp, it was a stark contrast to the life we had left behind. The camp was a makeshift community, with rows of homes constructed from whatever materials were available. Resources were scarce, and the challenges of daily survival tested our resolve. But within the confines of this small community, we discovered a remarkable spirit of cooperation and mutual support. We helped each other secure food, water, and shelter, sharing our resources and hopes and dreams for a brighter future.

Life in the camp was far from easy. We had to adapt to a new culture and learn a new language. Education became a beacon of hope, and many of us enrolled children in schools within the camp, determined to provide them with the opportunities we had been denied. We worked hard to sustain ourselves, becoming artisans, farmers, and teachers, contributing to the camp's self-sufficiency and fostering a sense of purpose and dignity in the face of adversity.

Despite the challenges and uncertainties that defined our refugee experience, our journey was not solely one of hardship. It was a journey marked by the indomitable human spirit. We celebrated weddings, births, and friendships that transcended borders and backgrounds. In the heart of this foreign land, we found a sense of belonging and community that gave us strength and hope.

It was a story of hope that transcended the borders of our homeland and embraced the possibilities of a new beginning. Through the challenges, sacrifices, and triumphs of our time in the M'porokoso camp, we learned that the human spirit could endure, even in the face of the most daunting circumstances. And as we built our lives anew, we carried with us the lessons of our journey—a testament to the power of hope, the strength of community, and the unwavering resilience of refugees.

Fleeing Home

Our journey as refugees began with the heart-wrenching decision to leave behind the land that had been our home for generations. The reasons behind our exodus were numerous and complex, but the devastating conflict that had torn our homeland apart was the driving force behind our departure. The conflict had not only shattered the tranquillity and safety we had once taken for granted but also disrupted our lives in unimaginable ways, leaving us with no choice but to flee.

The decision to abandon our homes, communities, and loved ones was not easy. It meant severing ties with the place that had witnessed our joys and sorrows, our dreams and aspirations. Leaving behind the familiarity of our surroundings, the warmth of our communities, and the comforting embrace of our loved ones was an indescribably painful process that left us with a profound sense of loss.

As we embarked on this daunting journey, we were filled with uncertainty and anxiety. We did not know what lay ahead or whether we would ever be able to return to our homeland. The road ahead was fraught with obstacles and challenges, and the terrain was unforgiving. Yet, with determination and hope as our steadfast companions, we persevered.

Our destination was Zambia, a nation that would soon become our new home. Zambia offered refuge, safety, and the promise of a fresh start. It was a place where we hoped to rebuild our lives, find solace amidst the chaos, and plant the seeds of a brighter future for ourselves and our families. The decision to make Zambia our new home was not taken lightly, but it was a choice driven by the pursuit of peace, stability, and the chance to begin anew.

We faced numerous challenges along the way, from navigating unfamiliar terrain to overcoming language barriers, but we remained steadfast in our determination to build a new life for ourselves.

Arrival in M'porokoso Camp

The radiant sun slowly descended below the horizon, casting a warm orange glow across the vast expanse of rugged terrain as our weary group of travellers came into view of M'porokoso Camp. This moment marked the end of an arduous journey fraught with danger, uncertainty, and an unrelenting pursuit of refuge. Despite our physical and emotional exhaustion, the sight of the camp was a welcome respite from the hardships we had faced.

Nestled deep within Zambia's Northern Province, M'porokoso Camp was a humble yet remarkable sanctuary to us and the countless others who had traversed the tumultuous path leading here. The camp, with its modest structures and basic amenities, may have seemed unremarkable to outsiders, but to us, it was a symbol of hope in a world plagued by chaos and despair.

The camp's location, amidst the stunning natural beauty of the region, provided us with a sense of solace and peace that we had not experienced in a long time. As we approached the camp, we could hear laughter and chatter, and the smell of cooking fires wafted toward us, filling our senses with a comforting aroma.

In that moment, we knew that we had found a place of refuge and safety, a place to rest and recharge, and a place to call home, even if only for a little while.

Our journey was a challenging one, full of difficulties and trials that tested our endurance and determination. We left everything familiar behind—our homes, loved ones, and secure lives—in pursuit of safety and a better future. At every step of the way, we faced danger, from the wilderness to treacherous terrain and uncertainty that seemed to loom at every turn.

As the days turned into weeks and the weeks into months, our group forged a bond born of shared hardship and hope. We had become a diverse tapestry of humanity, united by a common purpose—to find solace and sanctuary in M'porokoso. In our midst were families with children, elderly individuals who had witnessed the ebb and flow of countless seasons, and young souls yearning for a future untainted by the shadows of their past.

And so, it was on a day etched in our collective memory, the day when the distant outline of M'porokoso Camp first became visible on the horizon, that we felt a glimmer of hope piercing through the heavy shroud of despair that had hung over us for far too long. It was as if the universe had conspired to lead us to this place, this haven of safety and security nestled amidst the rugged beauty of Zambia's Northern Province.

Though modest in its physical appearance, the camp radiated an aura of reassurance. The first sight of its simple structures, surrounded by the natural beauty of the African landscape, brought tears to our eyes. We had endured countless trials, crossed formidable landscapes, and overcome unimaginable obstacles, all in the pursuit of reaching this very destination. In that moment, M'porokoso Camp was more than just a place; it was a symbol of our resilience, our indomitable spirit, and the unwavering hope that had carried us through the darkest hours.

The camp was a microcosm of humanity's capacity for compassion and cooperation. It housed individuals from various backgrounds, each with their own stories of hardship and survival. Some had fled conflict and persecution, seeking refuge in the warmth of its embrace. Others had embarked on arduous journeys, crossing vast distances and battling formidable odds, all with the shared dream of finding safety within these modest confines.

The community that had blossomed within M'porokoso was a true human spirit's ability to adapt and thrive, even in the face of adversity. It was a place where strangers became friends, shared meals symbolized solidarity, and children's laughter echoed through the air, providing a glimmer of hope in a world that often seemed harsh and unforgiving.

The camp's infrastructure may have been basic, with rows of humble dwellings constructed from locally sourced materials, but its significance was immeasurable. It was here that we found not only shelter from the elements but also a sense of belonging. It was a place where our stories were shared, our burdens lightened, and our dreams rekindled.

The surrounding landscape was a breathtaking backdrop to our daily lives. Rolling hills stretched as far as the eye could see, covered in lush greenery and dotted with vibrant wildflowers. The nearby river glistened in the sunlight, offering a source of sustenance and a place of serenity where we could reflect on our journey and our hopes for the future.

Life in M'porokoso was not without its challenges. The camp's resources were limited, and every day brought its own set of trials. Yet, it was precisely these challenges that fostered a sense of resilience and unity among its residents. Together, we cultivated the land, tended to our livestock, and worked tirelessly to ensure that everyone had enough to eat and a roof over their heads.

Community gatherings and cultural celebrations became cherished traditions within the camp. We shared our stories and traditions, forging a rich tapestry of cultures and experiences. Through song, dance, and storytelling, we found solace in our shared humanity, transcending the boundaries of language and background.

As the seasons cycled through their familiar patterns, we witnessed the transformative power of M'porokoso Camp. It was a place where individuals who had once been strangers became friends, where resilience turned adversity into strength, and where hope flourished in the face of uncertainty.

Our arrival in M'porokoso had not marked the end of our journey but rather the beginning of a new chapter in our lives. It was a chapter filled with challenges, yes, but also with the promise of a brighter tomorrow. The camp had become more than just a haven of safety; it had become a symbol of our shared determination to persevere, rebuild, and thrive.

As we gathered around crackling campfires in the quiet moments beneath the African stars, we reflected on our journey. We remembered the dangers we had faced, the trials we had endured and the uncertainty that had once clouded our path. But above all, we remembered the hope—the unwavering belief that had carried us through the darkest of nights and had led us to the welcoming embrace of M'porokoso Camp.

As we looked to the future, we knew that the challenges would continue, but so would our resilience. M'porokoso had become a place where dreams were nurtured, where friendships were forged, and where the human spirit shone brightest in the face of adversity. It was a haven of hope amidst the harshest of circumstances, a testament to the enduring power of community, compassion, and the unyielding belief in a better tomorrow.

Hope could prevail, and a new beginning could be found. And so, under the African sky, we embraced the challenges of each new day, grateful for the haven of safety and hope we had discovered in M'porokoso—a place that had not only welcomed us but had also rekindled the flicker of hope in our once-weary hearts.

UNHCR's Support in Mporokoso Refugee Camp: A New Beginning

The UNHCR is essential in providing support and assistance to my family living in Mporokoso refugee camp. The organization strives to offer a new beginning to those who fled their homes due to conflict, persecution, or other forms of violence. Mporokoso refugee camp, situated in the northern region of Zambia, served as a temporary home for thousands of refugees who fled their homeland due to conflict. We arrived at the camp with nothing but the clothes on our backs, traumatized by the violence and uncertainty we had left behind. The UNHCR provided a safe haven, ensuring our immediate protection and security upon arrival.

Security and Protection

UNHCR, in collaboration with the Zambian government and other partners, works tirelessly to ensure the safety and protection of refugees in Mporokoso. This includes providing security personnel to maintain order in the camp, monitoring for any potential threats, and addressing issues such as gender-based violence and child protection. UNHCR's presence remained instrumental in creating an environment where refugees begin to heal from the traumas of our past and rebuild their lives.

Shelter and Basic Necessities

One of the primary responsibilities of UNHCR in Mporokoso was to provide refugees with shelter and basic necessities upon arrival. Refugees were given tents and other temporary housing tools to protect them from danger. Additionally, UNHCR distributed food, clean water, and essential hygiene items to meet refugees' basic needs.

Access to healthcare is critical in any refugee camp, as many refugees arrive with various health issues resulting from their journey or the conditions they faced in their home countries. UNHCR ensured that healthcare services were readily available in Mporokoso, including clinics staffed by trained medical professionals. Regular health screenings, immunizations, and treatment for common illnesses were provided to refugees, ensuring that their health needs were met and enabling them to pursue a fresh start.

Once upon a time, in the heart of Mporokoso, a resilient community of refugees faced the daunting challenge of rebuilding their lives amidst the uncertainties of displacement. However, amidst the adversity, a glimmer of hope emerged through the unwavering efforts of UNHCR, which recognized the transformative power of education.

Education opportunities became the beacon of light for many in the refugee camp. The UNHCR understood that education was not just a classroom endeavor but a pathway to a brighter future. With determination, they strived to provide access to quality schooling within the camp's confines. Refugee children found solace in these makeshift classrooms, where they gained knowledge and a sense of normalcy and hope despite the challenging circumstances surrounding them.

But education did not stop with the children. The UNHCR recognized that refugees of all ages needed opportunities to learn and grow. Thus, they extended their support to vocational training and adult education programs. These initiatives equipped refugees with valuable skills, paving the way for self-reliance and a chance to rebuild their lives in the future.

The journey toward self-sufficiency didn't end there. UNHCR understood that true empowerment came from financial independence. Livelihood Support programs were introduced to help refugees generate income and stand on their own feet. These programs included vocational training, microfinance opportunities, and entrepreneurship training. Through these initiatives, refugees found the means to support themselves and their families, breaking free from the cycle of dependency.

Yet, the scars of displacement ran deep, and the psychological well-being of the refugees could not be overlooked. UNHCR recognized this, too. They offered psychosocial support services, staffed with trained counselors and mental health professionals. These heroes worked tirelessly, addressing the emotional and mental health issues that haunted the refugees. Through these support services, refugees embarked on a journey of healing and recovery, taking one step at a time toward rebuilding not just their lives but also their sense of self and hope for the future.

In the heart of Mporokoso, amid adversity, UNHCR's commitment to education, livelihood support, and psychosocial well-being ignited a flame of resilience and hope in the refugee community. Through the darkest of times, they found the strength to write their own stories of triumph over adversity, with the promise of brighter days ahead.

Community Building and Integration

In Mporokoso, where my heart is deeply invested, community building and integration are not just words; they are the very essence of hope. At UNHCR, they are committed to providing shelter and sustenance to refugees and are equally passionate about nurturing a sense of belonging and togetherness.

Imagine a place where refugees from diverse backgrounds come together as a family, sharing stories, laughter, and dreams. Refugees organize cultural events celebrating their differences, creating bonds that transcend borders and hardships. Through these initiatives, refugees are sowing the seeds of social cohesion, and every smile exchanged is a small victory for us. Together, we crafted a tapestry of unity in Mporokoso.

Legal Assistance and Documentation:

Amid uncertainty and displacement, legal assistance and documentation became lifelines for refugees. UNHCR stood by our side as we navigated the intricate web of legal processes. We were given documents that were not only pieces of paper; they were a passport to security and hope.

Picture a refugee family finally receiving the asylum status they have fought for or a young girl gaining access to the education she deserves through proper documentation. These moments were our greatest triumphs. UNHCR ensured that we had the legal status we needed to live and work in Zambia; we were not just given papers, but a future filled with possibilities.

Repatriation and Resettlement:

Mporokoso was not just a refugee camp but also a place where new beginnings were born. UNHCR's commitment doesn't end at providing shelter; it extends to creating pathways for refugees to rebuild their lives. When conditions improve in their home countries, UNHCR assists in their voluntary repatriation, helping them step back onto the soil they call home.

However, for those who cannot return due to continued conflict or persecution, UNHCER worked tirelessly to identify durable solutions. This included resettlement in third countries, where they can start anew in a safe and stable environment.

In Mporokoso, UNHCR was not just an organization; UNHCR was a beacon of hope, a bridge to a better tomorrow. UNHCR Staff was dedicated to building a vibrant, harmonious community, ensuring legal rights, and providing opportunities for refugees to find their way back to a life filled with dignity and security.

In Mporokoso refugee camp, UNHCR's support goes beyond meeting the immediate needs of refugees. It extends to empowering individuals and families to rebuild their lives and start anew. Through security, shelter, education, healthcare, and psychosocial support, UNHCR offers a holistic approach to addressing the challenges refugees face. By fostering self-reliance, promoting community integration, and facilitating legal processes, UNHCR played a crucial role in providing refugees in Mporokoso with the tools we needed to embark on a journey toward a brighter future. In doing so, UNHCR embodies the spirit of hope, resilience, and compassion, offering a new beginning to those forced to leave their homes behind.

Education

Education held a paramount significance within our family, transcending the confines of our challenging circumstances.

We resolved unequivocally that our pursuit of knowledge would remain unyielding, regardless of the adversities that encircled us. Amid the trials and tribulations of life in the camp, preserving our educational aspirations became the only hope to our strong determination.

Thanks to the benevolent support of international organizations, the camp authorities rose to the occasion. They established makeshift schools within the camp's confines to address the pressing need for education among the displaced populace. Although these schools were modest in appearance, they held immeasurable potential to reshape destinies and brighten futures.

These humble institutions, born from the collective resolve of both refugees and aid organizations, represented more than just classrooms. They were crucibles of transformation, symbolizing resilience and optimism. They served as conduits through which knowledge flowed, igniting the intellectual fires within the hearts and minds of countless individuals, including my family.

Within those makeshift classrooms, the spirit of curiosity and the hunger for learning thrived despite adversity. We discovered the boundless power of education, which became the compass guiding us toward a brighter future, not just for my family but for multitudes who shared our struggles. These schools nurtured dreams, cultivated talents, and instilled hope, proving that even in the harshest of circumstances, the pursuit of knowledge could illuminate the path to a more promising tomorrow.

Dreams and Aspirations

In the face of numerous difficulties and obstacles, we summoned the courage to envision a brighter future. Within the camp's confines, I stumbled upon a profound passion for storytelling and writing. Despite our meager resources, I sought refuge in the pages of books generously provided by humanitarian aid organizations. These books served as my gateway to the broader world, broadening my perspectives and fueling my aspirations for a more promising existence.

The Resilience of My Family in a Refugee Camp: A Story of Strength and Hope

Life in a refugee camp is a poignant testimony to the human spirit's ability to endure and overcome adversity. My family's journey in the camp was a profound experience, filled with challenges, hardships, illness, and loss, but it also illuminated humanity's indomitable spirit.

In the face of unimaginable difficulties, we found solace in the unexpected acts of kindness that flowed from fellow refugees and aid organizations' tireless efforts. These acts of kindness were like beacons of hope in our darkest hours, reminding us that compassion and empathy can thrive even in the bleakest of circumstances.

The resilience of the people in the camp left an indelible mark on our hearts. Our determination to rebuild our lives and protect our families was inspirational. We watched as they transformed makeshift tents into homes, turning barren land into communities of strength and support.

Our time in the refugee camp taught us invaluable lessons in gratitude, empathy, and perseverance. We learned to appreciate the small blessings we had, to be thankful for the sustenance and shelter we received, and to empathize with the countless others who shared our plight. These experiences forged a deeper connection with the global community, making us acutely aware of the interconnectedness of humanity and our shared responsibility to help one another in times of crisis.

Through it all, our family's resilience grew stronger. We discovered reservoirs of strength within ourselves that we never knew existed. We learned to adapt to the ever-changing circumstances and to hold onto hope even when it seemed elusive. The trials we faced in the refugee camp tested our resolve, but they also revealed the depths of our determination to create a better future for ourselves and those around us.

Ultimately, our time in the refugee camp was a chapter in our lives that we will never forget. It was a chapter marked by hardship and loss but also filled with hope, compassion, and the unbreakable bonds of family. We emerged from the camp with a newfound appreciation for the resilience of the human spirit, a commitment to making a positive difference in the world, and a belief that, even in the harshest of circumstances, there is always room for hope and healing.

Farewell to M'porokoso

It was an incredibly challenging and heart-wrenching experience for me to come to terms with the reality of my identity and the place I once called home - the Democratic Republic of Congo. The turmoil and devastation caused by wartime had shattered not only the physical structures but also the very foundations of my life.

The memories of that time are etched in my mind, haunting me with the stark images of destruction and persecution. I watched in helpless disbelief as our village, the place where I had spent my formative years, was mercilessly torn apart by bombs, reducing it to a mere shadow of its former self. The relentless fires of conflict swallowed the homes, the memories, and the sense of belonging.

In the aftermath of this devastation, a profound question echoed in my mind: How could I ever return to a place that had rejected not only me but also my family? I grappled with the painful realization that I no longer felt like a true Congolese citizen, yet I could not claim to be Zambian, either. I was trapped in a painful limbo, a state of identity crisis that left me feeling adrift in a world where I no longer belonged.

The loneliness that settled into my heart during those days was unlike anything I had ever experienced before. It was a profound sense of isolation that seemed impossible to convey in words. I yearned for a sense of belonging, a place where I could find solace and rebuild my life, but the path ahead seemed uncertain and fraught with challenges.

As time passed, I began to grapple with the complexities of my identity and the harsh realities of displacement. It was a journey filled with pain, resilience, and a burning desire to find a place where I could truly belong once more. Today, as I reflect upon those tumultuous times, I understand that my quest for a sense of home is not just a physical one but a journey to reclaim my identity and piece together the shattered fragments of my past.

Conversely, the day of our departure from M'porokoso refugee camp was an emotional rollercoaster, a poignant chapter in our lives coming to a close. We bid farewell to the friends and neighbours who had become our surrogate family over the past seven years. These people shared our joys, eased our sorrows, and offered unwavering support in our journey towards a better future. As we left, our hearts were heavy with gratitude for the sanctuary M'porokoso had provided.

M'porokoso had been our refuge from the storms of conflict and displacement. It had been a place where we found solace amidst the chaos of the outside world. The camp had offered us shelter, food, and a sense of security that was otherwise elusive in the tumultuous times we had left behind. But it was more than just a physical refuge; it was a community that embraced us, strangers in a foreign land, and turned us into a cohesive unit bound by shared experiences and dreams.

The friendships we forged in M'porokoso were unlike any other. They were forged in the crucible of adversity and hardship, strengthened by our collective determination to rise above our circumstances. We laughed together, cried together, and celebrated small victories as if they were monumental achievements. Children grew up together, their laughter echoing through the camp's dusty streets, reminding us of that life, even in the most trying conditions, could still be beautiful.

As we prepared to leave, tears welled up in our eyes. We were saying goodbye not only to the physical place but to the memories, the laughter, and the resilience that had defined our time in M'porokoso. The camp had been our home, our haven, and our anchor in uncertain times. It had been a place where we had learned to hope and dream again and found the strength to rebuild our lives.

But as we drove away from M'porokoso, we carried with us more than just memories. We carried the spirit of the camp, the resilience of its people, and the indomitable human spirit that had sustained us all those years. We were moving forward, stepping into a new chapter of our lives, but we knew that M'porokoso would forever be a part of us.

Farewell to M'porokoso was bittersweet, a farewell to a place that had sheltered us but also a tribute to the enduring bonds we had forged there. As we looked ahead, we knew that the lessons and the love we had found in M'porokoso would guide us in the years to come. We understood the human capacity for hope and the strength of community.

A Journey's End, a New Beginning

Our journey as refugees had come to a full circle, but it was not the end of our story. The experiences and lessons we learned in M'porokoso camp continued to shape our lives. We had gained a newfound appreciation for the value of community, education, and the resilience of the human spirit.

Challenges marked the seven years my family and I spent in M'porokoso camp, but they were also a pure test of the strength of our spirit. In the face of adversity, we discovered a sense of community, pursued education, and nurtured our dreams. Our journey as refugees was not just a story of survival; it was a story of hope, resilience, and the enduring power of refugees. Today, as we look back on those years, we are grateful for the sanctuary M'porokoso provided and the lessons it imparted. Our journey may have begun in hardship, but it continues with hope and determination to build a better future.

Meheba Settlement: A Legacy of Progress and Prosperity

Meheba Settlement was established in 1971 in the Kalumbila District, in the heart of the Northwestern Province of Zambia. Over the years, it has become an inspiring example of growth, development, and community resilience. With an area of 720 square kilometres, this district holds immense potential and opportunities, covering an area equivalent to the entire city-state of Singapore. Meheba Settlement has been carefully divided into many blocks, each contributing to this remarkable region's unique tapestry.

At the core of Meheba Settlement's success story lies its unwavering commitment to education and healthcare. The settlement has lots of high schools and basic schools that cater to the diverse needs of the local population. These institutions include community schools that have become the foundation of community engagement and empowerment—ensuring that community members, specifically the youth of Meheba Settlement, have access to the necessary tools for building brighter futures. In addition, the settlement clinics serve as a lifeline and provide essential medical care to those in need.

Safety and security are paramount in Meheba Settlement, exemplified by the presence of two police posts. These posts play a vital role in maintaining law and order, ensuring that the camp's residents can go about their daily lives with a sense of security and peace of mind.

Meheba Settlement is committed to supporting and caring for its most vulnerable members. The settlement's dedication to child protection is demonstrated through the presence of a center and safe houses, specifically for children at risk. These facilities offer refuge and support to children facing various forms of adversity, providing them with an opportunity for a brighter future. Furthermore, Meheba Settlement has established a center for women at risk, reaffirming its dedication to gender equality and the empowerment of women.

One of the most remarkable aspects of Meheba Settlement is the collaborative spirit that pervades its communities. Many different organizations that come to Meheba refugee camp represent diverse stakeholders and are actively implementing projects and assisting within the camp. These organizations contribute to the overall development and well-being of Meheba's residents. Their collective efforts highlight the shared commitment to progress and prosperity in Meheba.

The private sector has also played a significant role in driving economic growth and creating job opportunities in the region. Academic institutions have contributed to knowledge dissemination and skills development, ensuring that the residents of Mehaba are well-equipped to face the challenges of the modern world. Furthermore, individuals have been engaging in activities with passion and dedication, offering invaluable support and assistance to their fellow community members.

The journey of Meheba Settlement from its establishment in 1971 to its current status as a thriving community of opportunities and promises is a power of vision, collaboration, and resilience. Its success is not just about physical infrastructure; it is a story of people coming together to build a better future for themselves and future generations.

Refugees within Mehaba have played an indispensable role in its development. Their passion, dedication, and community spirit are the driving force behind many ad-hoc activities that address local challenges and meet the needs of their fellow refugees. Whether it is volunteering, mentorship, or simply lending a helping hand, individuals in Meheba Settlement have shown that collective action can lead to transformative change.

A Journey from Refugee to Renewal: My Life in Meheba Settlement

The day the news of repatriation was announced, the refugee camp I had called home for years buzzed with anticipation. We had spent a considerable portion of our lives in the safety of these camps, far from the conflicts and horrors of our home countries. Dreams of returning to our ancestral lands had filled our thoughts for years, and we believed the moment had finally arrived. Little did I know that the path to peace would take a different route.

In 2010, we faced the difficult decision of returning to our villages, a choice presented itself thanks to the intervention of the United Nations High Commissioner for Refugees (UNHCR). They offered an alternative for those of us who believed returning was still unsafe. This alternative was the Meheba settlement in the northwestern province of Zambia, approximately 4000 kilometres away from our previous homes in the M'porokose Mwange refugee camp. This decision was not made lightly, as it required us to weigh the risks and benefits carefully.

Ultimately, on July 12th, 2010, we decided to embark on a journey to this new haven called Meheba Settlement. It began a new chapter in our lives, one filled with hope, resilience, and determination. Over the next seven years, Meheba Settlement became our home, a place where we rebuilt our lives and sought refuge from the challenges we had left behind.

The decision to relocate us to Meheba Settlement in Zambia was met with a wave of confusion and uncertainty. Zambia, a country many of us had never even considered as a potential new home, was now our destination. It was a land we knew little about, apart from the fact that it was in Africa and relatively stable compared to our war-torn homelands. A sense of apprehension gripped me as we boarded buses bound for this unfamiliar land.

The journey to Meheba was a long and arduous one. We spent two full days on the road. The landscape shifted dramatically from the dense forests of the Congo to the open savannahs of Zambia. As the journey continued, so did my anxiety. Questions swirled in my mind. What would await me in Meheba? Would it be safe? Would we be able to rebuild my life there? When would I ever see my friends again? Was I born to be a refugee? Why me? Why my family?

Upon our arrival in Meheba Settlement, UNHCR Staff from the Solwezi office welcomed us with open arms. I was exhausted from sitting in the Markopolo bus that took over 48 hours to reach the northwestern province where we were going. It was a sprawling camp, much like the one we had left behind. Tents and small shelters dotted the landscape, and the sounds of children playing and adults conversing filled the air. The camp was a melting pot of cultures, languages, and stories on diverse backgrounds of its residents. We were no longer refugees from the Congo but a community of survivors, each with a unique tale of resilience.

One of the first things that struck me about Meheba was its sense of community. Despite our challenges, the people here had managed to forge deep bonds of friendship and support. We shared our stories and experiences, finding hope in the fact that we were not alone in our struggles. Meheba became more than just a settlement; it became a place of hope, healing, and unity.

Life in Meheba Settlement was not without its challenges. The conditions were basic, with limited access to clean water, healthcare, and education. We had to rely on the support of humanitarian organizations and the generosity of the Zambian government to meet our basic needs. Despite the hardships, the sense of community and the resilience of the people in Meheba carried us through.

The camp also had its share of success stories. As the years passed, my father started small businesses within the settlement, from small shops to food stalls. The entrepreneurial spirit that had been dormant for so long began to flourish once more. Meheba was not just a place of refuge; it was a place of rebirth.

I began to appreciate the beauty of Zambia as I settled into life in Meheba. The country's stunning landscapes, from the majestic Victoria Falls to the lush greenery of the Zambezi River, captivated my heart. The Zambian people were warm and welcoming, making us feel part of their extended family. The experience of living in Zambia broadened my horizons and gave me a deeper understanding of the richness of African culture.

Over time, I became involved in community initiatives to improve life in Meheba. Together with fellow residents, we advocated for better access to community services and youth education, reducing early parenthood in Meheba and around communities. These initiatives improved our quality of life and strengthened the bonds between us and the local population.

One of the most transformative experiences in Meheba was the opportunity to participate in vocational training programs. My journey as a child and youth care worker began in Meheba settlement. I will talk about that later in this book.

The years passed, and Meheba Settlement evolved. What was once a temporary refuge had become a semi-permanent home for many of us. Families grew, friendships deepened, and dreams of returning to our home countries faded. Instead, we started to dream of a different future, one that was built in Meheba.

In 2017, I had the privilege of witnessing a remarkable event. Meheba Settlement celebrated its 49th anniversary, a testimony of endurence spirit of its residents. The camp had come a long way from its humble beginnings, and the anniversary was a joyous occasion that brought the entire community together. It reminded us of how far we had come and how much we had achieved together.

As I reflect on my journey from refugee life to Meheba Settlement, I am filled with gratitude for the opportunities and experiences I have had. Meheba may not have been the destination I initially envisioned, but it has become a place where I found hope, resilience, and a sense of belonging. It is a place where I have witnessed the indomitable human spirit, where people from diverse backgrounds have come together to build a community against all odds.

My story is just one among the thousands that have unfolded in Meheba Settlement over the years. Each resident has a unique journey, trials, and triumphs. Together, we have turned Meheba into a place of hope, where dreams are rekindled and new beginnings are forged. Refugee life may have brought us here, but our determination and resilience have transformed Meheba into a place of renewal and possibility.

CHAPTER VI

LIFE IN BOARDING SCHOOL — MEHEBA BOARDING SCHOOL

Let's have a friendly chat about the Meheba boarding school system! Picture this: Meheba Refugee Settlement, nestled in Zambia, a place that has become a haven for people who have faced some tough times back in their home countries. Now, at the heart of this settlement, there's something really special— the Meheba boarding school.

Now, you might be wondering, "How does this school work?" Well, it's a place that welcomes students from all walks of life. Imagine Zambian and refugee kids coming together under one roof to learn and grow. It's like a little community of its own, where everyone brings their unique stories, languages, and experiences to the classroom.

Let's talk about how the school opens its doors to Zambian students who come from far and wide. You see, the school recognizes that education is for everyone, and they want to make sure that even if you're a Zambian student living a bit far from Meheba, you still get a chance to join this amazing community of learners.

So, the school has this welcoming process that makes it easy for Zambian students to enroll. There are paperwork and discussions with parents or guardians to understand the needs of the students. And before you know it, these Zambian students become part of the Meheba boarding school family.

Now, let's get into the classroom vibe. Can you imagine sitting in a class where you've got friends from all over— Zambia and different parts of the world? It's like a mini– United Nations of learning! You've got your Zambian pals sharing stories about their local culture, and then there are your refugee buddies, each with their rich backgrounds.

The school understands that language is a powerful tool for learning and connecting. That's why they've got this cool language support system. So, if you're a refugee or Zambian student and English is not your first language, no worries! The school has programs to help you catch up and feel at home. It's all about making sure everyone can participate and learn together.

Now, let me tell you about the magic in the classrooms. You've got teachers who are like guides on this learning adventure. They're there to help you understand new things, whether it's math, science, or language arts. And guess what? These teachers might include refugees themselves, bringing their own stories into the mix.

And here's the awesome part—the classrooms are places where friendships bloom. Zambian and refugee students sit side by side.

Fostering Holistic Development: The Boarding School Experience for Zambian and Refugee Students

In the pursuit of providing a nurturing educational environment, boarding schools play a crucial role in shaping the lives of both Zambian and refugee students. Let us explore the various aspects of boarding school life, emphasizing the importance of accommodation, daily routines, access to education, teaching staff, language support, extracurricular activities, healthcare services, vocational training, community involvement, and monitoring and evaluation.

Accommodation: One of the foundational elements of boarding school life is the provision of secure and stable living arrangements for students. Boarding facilities are meticulously organized to foster a sense of camaraderie among peers. Students arrive with their essentials packed in trunks, containing items ranging from food to clothes, ensuring they can fully immerse themselves in the learning experience without the need to return home throughout the semester.

Daily Routine: Structured routines define boarding school life, encompassing wake-up times, meals, study hours, and recreational activities. By striking a balance between academic pursuits and extracurricular engagements, students can develop holistically through these routines.

Access to Education: A paramount focus of boarding schools is prioritizing education. By accommodating students on-site, these institutions ensure easy access to classrooms, libraries, and other learning resources. This proximity fosters an immersive educational experience, enriching the academic journey.

Teaching Staff: Qualified teachers form the backbone of the boarding school experience, providing instruction across various subjects. Their expertise contributes significantly to the academic development of students, creating an environment conducive to learning.

Language Support: Acknowledging the linguistic diversity within the refugee population, boarding schools implement language support programs. These initiatives assist students who may not be proficient in the language of instruction, employing multilingual education strategies to bridge language gaps and enhance effective communication with Zambian students.

Extracurricular Activities: Beyond academics, extracurricular activities, such as sports, arts, and cultural events, are seamlessly integrated into the boarding school experience. These activities contribute to students' physical, emotional, and social well-being, fostering a sense of belonging and teamwork.

Healthcare Services: Prioritizing the health and well-being of students, boarding schools provide access to basic healthcare services within the settlement. Regular health check-ups and awareness programs address unique health challenges students face, ensuring a holistic approach to their welfare.

Vocational Training: Recognizing the importance of preparing students for self-sufficiency, vocational training programs are seamlessly integrated into the boarding school system. These initiatives equip students with practical skills, laying the foundation for their economic well-being and future success.

Community Involvement: The boarding school system actively encourages involvement from parents, guardians, and community leaders. This collaborative approach ensures a comprehensive student support network, fostering a sense of responsibility and shared commitment to their education and well-being.

Monitoring and Evaluation: To track students' academic progress, boarding schools implement regular assessments and evaluations. Robust data collection mechanisms monitor enrollment rates, attendance, and overall educational outcomes, enabling continuous improvement in the educational experience provided.

Meheba Boarding School System has some disadvantages for Zambian and Refugee Students

Limited Cultural Connection: Zambian students enrolled in the Meheba boarding school system often face disconnection from their cultural roots. The separation from their communities hampers the development of a strong cultural identity, impacting their sense of belonging and self-esteem.

Distance from Family: Boarding schools are typically located far away from students' homes. This geographical distance results in limited family visits, hindering emotional support and familial bonds crucial for a child's overall development.

Inadequate Individualized Attention: With a large number of students in boarding schools, individualized attention often takes a back seat. Refugees and Zambian students may struggle academically or emotionally without the personalized guidance needed for their unique academic needs and challenges.

Cultural Shock: Refugees, already dealing with the trauma of displacement, may find it challenging to adapt to the cultural norms within the boarding school system. The unfamiliar environment can exacerbate their sense of isolation and alienation.

Language Barriers: Many refugees in Zambia come from diverse linguistic backgrounds. The boarding school system might not adequately address language barriers, impacting the refugees' ability to engage in effective learning and social integration.

Limited Access to Resources: Refugees and Zambian students often face economic challenges, and the Meheba boarding school system may struggle to provide the necessary resources for students coming from economically disadvantaged backgrounds. This includes access to textbooks, educational materials, and extracurricular activities.

Personal Experience in Boarding School:

The boarding structure was as follows: Headmaster, vice-headmaster, accountant, staff, prefects, and dorm fathers and mothers. During the night, the prefect took care of the students and led them to the studding room after classes in the evening. We had cooks who were in charge of cooking the meals for hundreds of students who were in the boarding school. They cooked day and night to accommodate students with enough food.

In the heart of the boarding school experience, where regimented routines resembled a militarized existence, the struggle to survive wasn't limited to academic challenges alone. No, the true battleground lay within the confines of our dormitories, where the appointed prefects wielded a power that turned every aspect of life into a nightmarish ordeal.

Separated into male and female commotions, our existence within the sprawling school complex was a paradoxical blend of camaraderie and oppression. The day began in darkness, the ungodly hour of 5:00 a.m. heralding the commencement of our morning rituals. The first order of business was to clean the dorms and their surroundings, a precursor to the regimented line-up for breakfast. Little did we know that the supposed leaders appointed to guide and advise us would transform this routine into a series of torturous events.

As many would agree, boarding school is akin to a concentrated military camp. The nightly ritual of studying, an escape into the world of textbooks and knowledge, concluded at the stroke of 11:00 p.m. As the generator powered by electricity shut down, plunging the entire school into darkness, the teachers on duty activated the prefects, transforming them into ruthless enforcers.

These prefects, charged with maintaining order, descended upon the classrooms with an authoritarian zeal, herding students like cattle back to their respective dormitories. The darkness, thick with uncertainty, became a breeding ground for chaos. It wasn't about ushering us to our beds; it was a display of force and power that left us vulnerable to any harm lurking in the shadows.

As I stumbled back to my dormitory that fateful night, the dim light from my neighbor's bed revealed a scene of utter pandemonium. Grade 12 students, emboldened by their position, played music, engaged in shenanigans, and subjected the lower grades to a dehumanizing spectacle. The dormitories, meant to be sanctuaries of rest, became arenas of dominance, where the hierarchy was enforced with brutality.

I had just arrived in my dorm, and I was looking for my torch. I did not see it. With little light coming from my neighbour's bed, I noticed that my bag was missing. I wondered who would have taken my bag, which had all my school materials. Who could I have asked when everyone was busy thinking of themselves first? I gathered my courage and asked one of the prefects about my situation of my bad missing. Do you want to guess what I was told? In his angry voice, he said, "Go and steal too moreover, you Grade 10 students have the habit of complaining too much."

The corridors echoed with the cries of injustice, and the darkness held secrets that whispered of the cruelties inflicted upon us by those meant to guide and protect. In the confines of the boarding school, where camaraderie was tested and survival was paramount, the appointed leaders had become the architects of our torment. And as we navigated through the labyrinth of oppression, the night became a silent witness to the unravelling of our spirits, one stolen bag at a time.

As a refugee in Meheba, my days began early in a boarding school. Imagine this: before the sun even considered rising, at around 4:00 a.m., the boarding school prefect would appear armed with a slasher. Now, I want to be clear—there was no luxury of peacefully slumbering through this wake-up call. The slasher, a metal tool, became our unconventional alarm clock.

Now, you might be wondering, how does a slasher wake someone up? Well, here's the thing: both the slasher and our beds were made of metal. Just think about the noise two pieces of metal can create when they collide. The boarding prefect would make an entrance, brandishing the slasher, and start banging it against the metal bed stand. The resulting clatter was enough to jolt anyone awake, even if you were in the deepest sleep imaginable.

If the metallic symphony failed to rouse certain heavy sleepers, alternative wake-up strategies were on standby. Picture this: a bucket of ice-cold water being unceremoniously poured onto the bed. Their defense? A reluctance to waste precious early morning energy on mere words.

But that wasn't the end of it. In the hierarchy of unconventional wake-up techniques, there was the extreme approach. Another prefect might arrive armed with a potentially harmful weapon, ready to deliver swift blows to anyone in the land of dreams, indifferent to where the impact landed. In this world, the unspoken rule was clear—actions spoke louder than words.

So, I was navigating the dawn of each day in this peculiar routine. The clash of metal, the shock of cold water, and the occasional strike from a forceful weapon were not just disruptions but the raw language of survival. In the corridors of a boarding school where words seemed to fail, actions became the powerful expression of our shared experiences and the unyielding strength required to face each new day as a student in boarding school.

There were countless mornings when I dutifully followed all the rules—waking up at the crack of dawn, enduring the cacophony around me, and meticulously tending to my chores. But my heart sank when I finally made my way to grab a bite for breakfast. The food was gone, vanished, leaving me with an empty stomach and a heavy heart.

Sometimes, it was the fault of the cooks who failed to prepare enough for the day. Other times, it was the excruciating wait in line until 7:30 am, only to be told that orders had ceased, and we had to scurry off to class on an empty stomach. The hunger pangs were real, and the frustration even more palpable.

In the worst scenarios, a prefect—the enforcer of order— would deliver a blow to our hunger. I remember one morning vividly when a prefect sternly warned me not to set foot in the dining area. Why? Because I had refused to offer him my precious bucket of water from a water pump, which took me about twenty minutes to wait.

It was a tough pill to swallow—waking up early, enduring hunger, and facing arbitrary rules. Each morning presented a new challenge, a test of resilience in the face of hunger and authority. Yet, despite the hardships, we pressed on, driven by the simple desire for a nourishing meal and a fair shake in the dining hall.

The community played an essential role throughout my time in boarding school at Meheba High School. Parents and guardians were encouraged to actively participate in my education, attending meetings and supporting my learning journey. Community leaders and volunteers were also involved in creating a supportive and collaborative educational environment.

The boarding school experience is not just about academics; it's a holistic approach to your development, considering my unique background and needs. The goal is to provide me with the skills, knowledge, and resilience needed to face the challenges of the present and build a better future despite the adversities I may have encountered in my home country.

While the Meheba boarding school system aims to provide education and opportunities for a brighter future, it is essential to acknowledge and address the disadvantages it presents to both Zambian students and refugees. Balancing the benefits of education with the need for cultural preservation, family connections, and personalized support is crucial for creating a more inclusive and effective educational environment for all.

CHAPTER VII

WORKING WITH REFUGEES IN MEHEBA

My story is evidence of the strength and resilience of individuals who find themselves in challenging and unforeseen circumstances. In 2003, many parts of the world experienced conflicts, natural disasters, and other crises that forced people to become refugees, and my experience sheds light on the hardships and triumphs that often come with a journey.

My journey from becoming a refugee to working with other refugees in Meheba Settlement, Zambia, is undoubtedly a remarkable one. Working with fellow refugees in a settlement demonstrates a sense of compassion and solidarity that is often crucial in such environments.

It's essential to acknowledge the challenges refugees face, including displacement, loss of home, community, and, often, personal possessions. The journey is filled with uncertainty, fear, and the need to adapt to new cultures and environments. My determination and resilience, however, allowed me to survive and thrive and contribute positively to the community I became a part of.

My story highlights the importance of supporting and helping refugees as they seek to rebuild their lives. It's also a reminder of the potential for personal growth and fulfillment in even the most challenging situations. By sharing my story, I am not only inspiring others but also raising awareness about the experiences of refugees, fostering greater understanding and empathy in the wider world.

Indeed, being a refugee is a significant and life-altering experience that is marked by numerous challenges and hardships. Refugees are forced to leave their homes and countries due to a wide range of reasons, including danger, conflict, persecution, natural disasters, or other life-threatening circumstances. These individuals often face a perilous journey to find safety and a better future.

Several key aspects mark the experience of being a refugee:

Forced Displacement: As a past refugee, I did not choose to leave my home willingly. I was forced to flee because staying in my home country was no longer safe or viable.

Loss and Trauma: Leaving behind one's home, possessions, and often loved ones can be an incredibly traumatic experience. I endured loss and hardship during my journey.

Legal Status: I was granted refugee status because refugees have a distinct legal status under international law, as defined by the 1951 Refugee Convention. This status was crucial for my protection and rights in the host country.

Seeking Safety: My primary motive for becoming a refugee was to seek safety and protection from persecution or danger. This search for safety often involves crossing borders and navigating complex legal and bureaucratic processes.

Integration Challenges: Once in a host country, I remember facing numerous challenges in terms of integration, including language barriers, cultural differences, and the need to rebuild my life from scratch.

Aspirations for a Better Future: I hung on to hope for a better future for myself and my family. I kept dreaming and seeking opportunities for education, work, and a life free from the threats we face in Congo DRC, our home country.

It's important for individuals, communities, and nations to understand the plight of refugees and offer support when possible. Empathy and compassion are crucial in helping refugees rebuild their lives and find a sense of security and belonging in their new homes.

My own journey as a refugee began in circumstances beyond my control. The specifics of my departure from my home may differ from those of other refugees, but our emotions and challenges are often strikingly similar. We all share a common thread of leaving behind our lives, our homes, and our sense of belonging in search of safety and hope. This is a universal experience that transcends borders, cultures, and backgrounds, uniting us in our shared quest for a better life.

The destination for my new chapter as a refugee was the Meheba Settlement, nestled in the northwestern part of Zambia. This settlement served as a sanctuary for countless individuals and families, all seeking refuge from the storms of conflict and uncertainty. It is a place where we could find shelter, support, and a sense of community amidst the chaos and displacement that had become our reality.

My story isn't just about the difficulties of being a refugee; it's about the unwavering determination to make the most of this situation and to offer help to others facing similar challenges. In the face of adversity, I made a conscious choice to become actively involved in supporting fellow refugees within the Meheba Settlement. This decision wasn't just a personal one; it was driven by the understanding that together, we could overcome the hurdles and emerge stronger.

Life in a refugee settlement is far from easy. The daily struggles to secure food, clean water, and basic necessities are a constant reminder of the hardships we endure. The unfamiliar surroundings, the language barriers, and the sense of displacement create a daunting backdrop to our lives. Yet, within this challenging environment, I discovered a powerful source of strength: the indomitable human spirit.

As a helping hand to my fellow refugees, I quickly realized the transformative power of unity. Together, we could provide support to those who needed it most. We formed bonds that transcended our differences and celebrated our shared resilience. In helping others, I found purpose and a renewed sense of hope.

My role within the Meheba Settlement evolved from that of a newcomer to an advocate for change. I became involved in community projects, assisting in the construction of basic infrastructure, advocating for access to education, and promoting gender equality. By working together, we improved the living conditions in the settlement and provided opportunities for self-improvement. These efforts benefited the refugee community and fostered understanding and cooperation with the local Zambian population.

The journey was not without its setbacks and challenges. I witnessed the anguish of families torn apart, the despair of those who had lost everything, and the emotional scars that war and persecution leave behind. However, these experiences only fueled my determination to make a difference. I realized that by sharing our stories and our dreams, we could inspire one another and remind ourselves that a better future was within our grasp.

Meheba Settlement became a microcosm of hope within the larger context of global displacement. It taught me that the human spirit can prevail even in the most challenging circumstances, and individuals can come together to create positive change. We may have been refugees, but we were also builders, dreamers, and advocates for a brighter tomorrow.

My journey as a refugee ultimately led me to appreciate the profound resilience of fellow refugees. It showed me that hope can thrive in the most unlikely of places and that a sense of belonging can be found in the most unexpected communities. Our shared experiences, though marked by hardship, transformed us into a network of support and willingness to assist one another.

While my journey as a refugee began in circumstances beyond my control, it allowed me to embrace my role as a helping hand to others who faced similar trials. Amid uncertainty, we found purpose in supporting one another. Refugees are bound by the belief that a better tomorrow is possible despite the challenges they face.

In Meheba Settlement, I discovered that the power of unity and collective action could transform lives. It reinforced the idea that, even in the darkest times, people have a glimmer of hope when they come together with a common purpose. My experience as a refugee and my subsequent efforts to assist fellow refugees have illuminated the strength that can emerge from adversity and the enduring human spirit that refuses to be extinguished.

As I reflect on my journey, I am reminded of the countless individuals and families who continue to seek refuge around the world. The global refugee crisis is an ongoing challenge, and the stories of those forced to flee their homes are as diverse as the world itself. Yet, at the heart of each of these stories is a common thread of resilience, the pursuit of a better life, and the yearning for a sense of belonging.

My journey as a refugee has forever shaped my perspective on the world. It has shown me that the human bond can rise above, find strength in unity, and create a better future in the face of adversity. While my path may have been marked by displacement, it is also marked by hope, resilience, and the unwavering belief that we can build a more inclusive and compassionate world for all.

Pursuing a Dream: My Journey from Admiring UNHCR Workers to Aspiring to Join Their Ranks

As a child, I was always inspired by the stories of resilience, compassion, and dedication I heard about UNHCR workers. Their strong commitment to providing aid and support to refugees and displaced populations around the world left an indelible mark on my young mind. This admiration for UNHCR workers became the driving force behind my academic aspirations, propelling me towards a future where I could potentially become a part of this remarkable organization. Let me share my journey of how my admiration for UNHCR workers led me to pursue an education with the goal of joining their ranks.

As I was growing up, my awareness of the UNHCR and its vital work was shaped by both my family's discussions and the media. My parents often discussed global issues at the dinner table, including conflicts, displacement, and humanitarian crises. They would share stories of UNHCR workers who risked their lives to provide aid to those in need. These stories painted a picture of brave individuals who selflessly devoted themselves to a cause greater than themselves.

The media's coverage of humanitarian crises around the world frequently featured the efforts of UNHCR workers. Whether through documentaries, news articles, or interviews, I was exposed to the selflessness and dedication of these individuals who worked tirelessly to alleviate the suffering of refugees and displaced persons. The images of UNHCR workers distributing food, setting up shelters, and offering a glimmer of hope in dire circumstances left an indelible impression on me.

As I entered my teenage years, my admiration for UNHCR workers evolved into a desire to follow in their footsteps. I began to research the organization more thoroughly, learning about its mission, values, and impact on the lives of millions. It became clear to me that education would be a crucial step on my path toward potentially joining UNHCR.

With this newfound determination, I set out on a rigorous academic journey with the organization's ideals always in my mind. My goal was clear: to complete my education and equip myself with the knowledge and skills necessary to contribute to the noble cause of helping refugees and displaced people. The road ahead was challenging, but I was motivated by the belief that every small step I took in my academic journey would bring me closer to realizing my dream.

In high school, I focused on courses and extracurricular activities that aligned with my long-term goals. I took an active interest in subjects like leadership and foreign languages, which I knew would be valuable for a future career with UNHCR. Additionally, I volunteered with local organizations that supported refugees in our community Mwange Mporokoso refugee camp, which allowed me to gain firsthand experience in working with displaced populations. These experiences only reinforced my determination to work with UNHCR in the future.

In addition to academics, I sought out internships and volunteer opportunities that would allow me to gain practical experience. I interned with a non-governmental organization that collaborated closely with UNHCR, and I also volunteered with various humanitarian initiatives. These experiences gave me valuable insights into the challenges faced by refugees and the complexity of humanitarian work. They also provided me with opportunities to interact with professionals who had worked directly with UNHCR, further solidifying my aspiration to be part of their team.

As graduation approached, I knew it was time to take the next step toward realizing my dream. I began researching UNHCR's recruitment processes, requirements, and available positions within my refugee camp. I was not successful in securing a job. I felt lost and disappointed. I took on a heavy driving career, but working with UNHCR was still winning and signing in my brain.

The waiting period that followed was filled with anticipation and nervousness. I knew that competition for positions at UNHCR was fierce, and many talented individuals aspired to be a part of the organization. However, my journey had been driven by a genuine passion for the cause and a determination to make a difference. I believed my dedication would shine through in my application.

As the days turned into weeks, I received word of mouth from a UNHCR worker who knew me. It was an invitation for an interview. The excitement and gratitude I felt were indescribable. This was the moment I had been working towards for years, and I was now one step closer to my dream of joining UNHCR.

The interview process thoroughly evaluated my qualifications, skills, and commitment to UNHCR's mission. I was interviewed by a panel of experienced UNHCR professionals who questioned me on my understanding of humanitarian work, my ability to adapt to challenging environments, and my willingness to work with children from war zone places. They asked me why I wanted to work with refugee children and what that meant to me; they asked me how I would make a difference in the lives of these children. It was a challenging interview, but I felt a strong connection with the organization's values and goals, and I answered every question with sincerity and conviction.

The waiting period after the interview was nerve-wracking, but I remained hopeful. Finally, I was shortlisted among 32 newly hired young men in the Meheba settlement. We were recruited and the plan was to train us to become child and youth care workers. It was an offer of employment from UNHCR in partnership with the National Association of Child and Youth Care Workers (NACCW) from South Africa. I had been selected to join the team as a child and youth care worker, and we were to work within Meheba Settlement. The joy was on top of everything in my life.

When I completed my training, tears of joy rose in my eyes. It was the realization of my dream becoming true. I joined UNHCR Meheba as a Child and Youth Care Worker (CYCW). I can certainly agree that the more we work hard, the more we make this world a better place to live.

In life, it's important never to give up, no matter how many times you fail. Instead, try your best to fall forward. This way, you'll be able to see where you're going wrong and figure out how to pick yourself up and keep going. Consistent discipline is key to achieving your goals. It's not a one-time thing, but rather, a daily effort to improve the areas where we struggle. It's important to remember that success is not something that happens overnight but rather requires consistent effort over time. It's crucial to keep pushing forward, even when things get tough, in order to achieve your goals.

It is crucial to keep in mind that being busy doesn't equate to making progress. Don't confuse mere "movement" with actual progress. Genuine progress comes from learning, growing, and working hard to create a meaningful impact. To achieve success, you must be willing to take risks and step out of your comfort zone. Remember, even the most successful people have to take risks to get where they are.

People often say going to college or university is a good idea because it provides something to fall back on. However, I've never really understood this concept of having a backup plan. If I'm going to fall, I don't want to fall back on something—I want to fall forward. At least that way, I'll be able to see where I'm going and what I'm about to hit. Falling forward means embracing failure and learning from it, no matter how many times you stumble. Each failure can teach you valuable lessons that will help you move forward in your journey toward success.

Remember that every failure is a valuable lesson that can lead you to success. Taking risks in life is necessary, even if it means facing embarrassment, challenges, or losing. The key is to fall forward and learn from your experiences. You can also gain insights from people around you by observing their successes, failures, and differences. Allow others to help you as you move forward in your journey.

I tried a thousand times to succeed in school and reach my career goals, and a thousand times, I failed. But I never gave up. My struggles and failures as a youth led me to become a child and youth care worker. Through my work, I was able to positively impact my community by providing a safe space for community members, emotional health, and academic advancement.

My failures have taught me to recognize and address the needs of my community. Together, we can stand as one family of brothers and sisters and make this world a better place. Let's hold each other's hands and lift each other up as we fall forward together.

Before scooping a position as a CYCW, I remember interviewing with a certain wholesale in town for a maintenance position. However, I didn't pass the interviews. But failures can be learning experiences. Humility is recognizing, reflecting on, and learning from your mistakes. It's falling forward. After that interview, I fell forward and became a Child and Youth Care worker at UNHCR offices. I advocated for orphans and vulnerable children in my community to have access to education, food, clothing, and shelter. They were able to live well and become the next generation and caretakers of our planet.

To fall forward, you need to try new things and be ready to fail. If you're not uncomfortable, you're not growing. Although it may take years to achieve your goals, remember that taking shortcuts can lead to shorter achievements and a longer path to success. Take the hard road, learn new things, and be different.

Never be discouraged. Never hold back. And when you stumble, remember to fall forward. To all the people you meet in your life, thank them for the gifts they've shared with you and what you've learned from them. Be grateful for helping you discover something within yourself. This is how I choose to live my life, and it's the reason why I'm happy today and am who I am.

If you ever get to a place where you feel successful, it's a good time to give back and take the hand of someone in your community, school, or wherever you are. Teach that person how you flourished and achieved your wonderful goals.

Let's come together and promote kindness and togetherness and uphold the values of humanity. By working shoulder to shoulder and strengthening our community, we can help and grow each other. Today, many people have worked tirelessly to bring joy and happiness to others. Child and youth care workers have also done their part by working with children from their homes and schools, ensuring they don't get caught in the vicious cycle of poverty.

I began working in Meheba Camp, an impoverished area that made me feel unsafe. Because I believed my stammer might be a hurdle, I listened attentively and learned from the individuals I was trying to assist. This proved to be a valuable asset to my career. As a humanitarian worker, the role requires diverse skills, and I received supervision from highly-trained individuals from the National Association of Child and Youth Care Workers (NACCW) and the Zambia Association of Child and Youth Care Workers (ZACCW).

Working with orphans, children, and youth in a refugee context can be challenging. Here are some important considerations I took to make my work successful.

Reflected on My Experiences: I kept reflecting on my own experiences as an orphan and a refugee. This self-awareness helped me better understand the needs and challenges of the children I worked with.

Mentorship: Seek out mentors who are experienced in humanitarian work, especially those who have worked with refugee populations. They provided valuable guidance and insights.

Specializing in Trauma-Informed Care: Given the experiences of many refugee children, I was trained in trauma-informed care. This equipped me with the skills to address the unique emotional and psychological challenges refugee children face.

Advocacy and Awareness: I used my personal story and my work to advocate for the rights and well-being of refugee children. Raising awareness about their needs and issues is a crucial part of being a humanitarian.

Cultural Competency Training: I continued to educate myself on the cultures, languages, and traditions of the children I served. This helped me build trust and connect with them more effectively.

Community Building: I created a supportive and welcoming community for the children I worked with. This included support groups, mentorship programs, and safe spaces where they could share their experiences.

Collaborate: I collaborated with other organizations within Mehaba to ensure the support provided was easily accessible through referrals to other organizations. I strongly believe in working together, which can amplify the skills of the people we are supporting and leave a lasting impact on the community.

Evaluation and Learning: Regularly, I assessed our programs and initiatives to see what was working and what could be improved. I was always open to feedback from the children and youth I was helping.

Self-Care: As I continued to support others, I did not forget to prioritize self-care to ensure I was in a healthy mental and emotional state to provide support effectively.

My journey and commitment to being a role model for orphaned and refugee children will make a significant difference in the lives of many. To date, I keep pursuing my passion and adapting to different approaches as needed to serve these vulnerable populations better.

In the heart of Meheba settlement, where the echoes of resilience are louder than the struggles, I continued on a journey to understand and address the intricate needs of refugees. Conducting a profound needs assessment became the compass guiding this expedition, a journey marked by collaboration, advocacy, and a relentless pursuit of restoring dignity to those who had lost so much.

Collaboration emerged as the cornerstone of my approach. Recognizing the complexity of the challenges faced by refugees, I sought to weave a tapestry of support by establishing partnerships with local authorities, UN agencies, and NGOs. This collaborative effort became a collective strength and compassion that could be harnessed when diverse stakeholders unite for a common cause. Together, we envisioned a harmonious symphony of aid and empowerment echoing through the settlement.

Advocacy became my voice in this symphony, a melody of compassion resonating for the vulnerable souls seeking refuge. Shelter and healthcare services emerged as the focal points of my advocacy efforts. Every child and every family deserves the basic human right to a safe and secure dwelling. Through tireless advocacy, I ensured that refugee children, with their innocent eyes reflecting dreams of a brighter future, found solace in shelters that echoed with the warmth of compassion.

Healthcare, too, became a sanctuary for healing. Advocating for access to healthcare services became more than a professional duty; it became a pledge to safeguard the well-being of those who had endured the harsh winds of displacement. In every consultation room, the whispered hopes of refugees intertwined with the commitment to provide holistic care, fostering a healing environment that transcended mere medical assistance.

In education, my advocacy assumed the guise of a call for enlightenment and empowerment. I fervently advocated for school sponsorship programs, recognizing that education is the beacon that illuminates the path toward a better tomorrow. Every child deserves the chance to learn, dream, and cultivate the skills that would empower them to rebuild their shattered lives.

The theme of empowerment extended into the legal arena, where I endeavored to be a beacon of guidance for refugees navigating the intricate legal landscape. Understanding one's legal rights became a cornerstone in the journey toward reclaiming agency and dignity. Through legal support and aid, we aimed not only to assist in legal matters but also to empower refugees with the knowledge that they were not alone in their pursuit of justice and security.

In the midst of Zambian bureaucratic complexities, my commitment to advocating for the most vulnerable remained unwavering. Legal aid became a lifeline, a bridge connecting the displaced to a sense of justice, no matter how far they had traveled from home.

Community Building: In my commitment to fostering a sense of community and social cohesion, I prioritize initiatives that bring refugees together. Through cultural events, workshops, and collaborative projects, I aimed to strengthen the bonds among community members. By promoting a shared sense of identity and purpose, I believe we can alleviate the isolation often experienced by refugees.

Child Protection: Recognizing the vulnerability of refugee children, UNHCR's program includes a dedicated Child

Protection component. We take immediate action when a child is referred to us, whether by a nearby department or through our community outreach. Our focus is on creating a protective environment, ensuring the child's safety and well-being through tailored interventions. This includes access to educational resources, psychosocial support, and collaboration with relevant authorities to address any legal or guardianship issues.

Our holistic approach extends beyond these core components. We understand that a secure and supportive community is essential for the overall well-being of its members, especially children. By combining community-building activities with child protection measures, we strive to create a resilient, nurturing environment that empowers refugees to overcome challenges and build a better future.

Together, we can make a lasting impact by fostering a community that survives and thrives, where every individual, especially every child, is allowed to grow and flourish despite the adversities they may face.

CHAPTER VIII

YOU ARE NOT A REFUGEE—IT IS JUST A NAME

Are you feeling a bit perplexed when you encounter the term "refugee"? Do you find it a daunting, imposing word that seems to carry the weight of defining your identity? Well, let's embark on a journey to demystify this term with plain and straightforward language. You are not a refugee; it's merely a label that holds no sway over your inherent value or your identity as an individual.

To begin, let's establish a clear understanding of what a refugee truly is. A refugee is someone who has been compelled to abandon their place of origin due to deeply distressing circumstances such as wars, violence, or natural disasters. Importantly, it's not a choice they made; it's a necessity forced upon them. Think of it like having to leave a game that has become neither enjoyable nor secure. Refugees are similarly left with no choice because their departure is driven by a very real fear for their lives and their safety.

These individuals are like you or me. They share the same fundamental desire for a peaceful and secure existence. They may have been teachers, doctors, artists, or students in their homelands, pursuing their dreams and living their lives just like you. However, the harrowing circumstances in their home countries have forced them to leave behind the lives they cherished, just as you might leave a playground when danger lurks.

In essence, being a refugee does not reflect one's worth, character, or potential. It is a status that describes a chapter in their lives, a phase marked by resilience, strength, and the hope for a brighter future. Like you, they are individuals who yearn for safety, happiness, and opportunities to thrive.

Remember, the term "refugee" doesn't encompass the entirety of who you are as a person. It's an aspect of one's journey, but it doesn't define your worth or the incredible potential within you. So, the next time you encounter this term, you can look beyond it and see the unique human stories, hopes, and dreams that it represents.

Being called a refugee doesn't diminish your worth or humanity; it's simply a term used to describe the challenging journey and experiences you've faced. It's crucial to understand that this label does not define your character, your abilities, or your potential to achieve remarkable things. In the grand narrative of life, you remain inherently you, with all your exceptional qualities and the endless possibilities that lie ahead.

The term "refugee" often carries with it a heavy weight, laden with misconceptions and stigmas. Yet, it is essential to remember that labels are but superficial markers, unable to capture the depth and breadth of a person's identity and potential. To be a refugee means to overcome tremendous adversity, displaying a resilience and strength that few others can comprehend. Your journey is your true confirmation to your determination, and your experiences have undoubtedly shaped you into a unique and remarkable individual.

It's important to acknowledge that everyone has a story, a past that has contributed to their present. While being a refugee is part of your story, it does not overshadow the multitude of other elements that define you. Your skills, talents, and dreams remain as vibrant and significant as anyone else's. This label should not limit your aspirations but empower you to embrace your dreams with the same fervour and ambition as anyone else.

Your skills are a testament to your abilities, honed through the challenges you've faced. As a refugee, you have likely had to adapt to new environments, cultures, and languages. This adaptability is an incredible skill that speaks to your capacity for learning and your ability to thrive in unfamiliar circumstances. Your life experiences have cultivated a unique perspective that enriches your understanding of the world, a perspective that can contribute to innovation and problem-solving in ways that others might not envision.

Your dreams are equally as important and valid as anyone else's. The label of a refugee should not impose limitations on your aspirations. Instead, it should serve as a reminder of the hurdles you've already conquered and the strength that resides within you. The dreams you hold are the compass that guides you toward a future filled with purpose and fulfillment.

In pursuing these dreams, it's essential to recognize that greatness knows no boundaries. History is replete with stories of individuals who rose from adversity to achieve incredible feats. Your past does not bind your potential; the fire of your determination illuminates it. Regardless of where you come from, your potential to bring about positive change in your life and the lives of others is boundless.

Moreover, your unique qualities are an integral part of your identity. Every person is a tapestry of distinct attributes, experiences, and perspectives. Your uniqueness is a gift that enriches the world. It's your individuality that can lead to the creation of art, the discovery of new solutions, and the forging of connections between people and cultures. Embrace your uniqueness, for it is a source of strength and inspiration that can inspire and connect profoundly with others.

Your heritage, your language, and your experiences are all facets of your identity that contribute to your individuality. They provide a rich tapestry of stories and wisdom you can share with the world. By sharing your experiences, you have the power to educate and enlighten, fostering empathy and understanding among those who may not have walked the same path. Your unique perspective has the potential to break down barriers and promote a more inclusive and compassionate world.

In the journey of life, labels such as "refugee" are but brief chapters in a much larger narrative. Your story is still being written, and the future holds limitless opportunities. It's crucial to recognize that you are not alone in this journey. Many people and organizations are dedicated to supporting refugees and helping them rebuild their lives. Seek out these resources, for they can provide guidance, education, and the tools to help you achieve your dreams.

In addition to external support, it's vital to cultivate self-compassion and self-belief. Acknowledge your own resilience and strength. Understand that, as a refugee, you have already faced challenges that would deter many. Use this knowledge to bolster your self-confidence. Recognize that, despite the obstacles, you are continually moving forward and making progress. This inner strength is a wellspring of power that can help you overcome any hurdles in your path.

As you continue to pursue your dreams and aspirations, remember that every step you take is a victory, no matter how small. Your journey may have started with hardship and adversity but is evolving into a story of triumph and resilience. Celebrate your achievements, no matter how minor they may seem, and use them as stepping stones to reach greater heights. Your progress is a true path to your unwavering determination and your refusal to be defined by circumstances beyond your control.

Let's look at a few reasons why being called a refugee doesn't define you:

Strength and Resilience:

A refugee's journey is often marked by adversity and hardship, but through these trials, they showcase remarkable strength and resilience. As you navigate this arduous path, it's crucial to recognize and celebrate the incredible qualities that make you truly amazing.

The life of a refugee is a story of upheaval and uncertainty. Forced to flee their homes due to conflict, persecution, or other perilous circumstances, they embark on a journey into the unknown. Leaving behind everything they once knew and loved, refugees find themselves in a foreign land, struggling to build a new life. Their challenges are numerous and profound, from language barriers to cultural differences and economic instability to the absence of a support system.

Despite these formidable obstacles, refugees demonstrate an extraordinary level of resilience. This inner strength, forged through adversity, is a source of inspiration to refugees and the world at large. The ability to endure unimaginable hardships and still carry hope in one's heart is nothing short of remarkable.

One of the most remarkable aspects of refugees' resilience is their adaptability. As a refugee, you have likely had to learn new languages, navigate complex bureaucratic systems, and adjust to unfamiliar customs and traditions. These adjustments require a remarkable level of flexibility and a willingness to embrace change. Your capacity to adapt and thrive in an entirely new environment showcases the indomitable spirit that resides within you.

Also, the experience of being a refugee often instills in individuals a deep appreciation for the simple joys of life. Basic necessities like safety, shelter, and sustenance become profound blessings. Your ability to find happiness amid such simplicity is a true attestation to your character. This newfound perspective can serve as a source of inspiration to those who have never experienced the same hardships.

Refugees' resilience is also reflected in their ability to rebuild their lives from scratch. Starting anew in a foreign land is a daunting task, but it is one that you have taken on with courage and determination. From finding employment to securing housing, building a social network, and pursuing education, each step forward demonstrates your unwavering commitment to a better future.

In addition to their resilience, refugees possess a sense of unity and community that is truly exceptional. In the face of adversity, many refugees come together to support one another, forming tight-knit communities. These communities offer practical assistance and emotional support, creating a sense of belonging in a foreign land.

Refugees' journeys are often marked by uncertainty and unpredictability. The prospect of returning to one's home or being resettled in a new country can be uncertain and filled with challenges. Yet, you persist in the face of these obstacles, and this persistence is a remarkable trait that distinguishes you. The ability to endure the unknown and maintain hope for a better future is nothing short of extraordinary.

Your resilience and strength as a refugee are truly something to be proud of. The challenges you have faced have shaped you into an amazing individual. Your adaptability, your appreciation for the simple joys of life, your capacity to rebuild, your sense of community, and your ability to persevere through uncertainty all make you an inspiration to those around you.

Refugees have indeed faced unimaginable challenges, and we can truly appreciate your remarkable strength and resilience. Your journey, marked by adversity and uncertainty, demonstrates your adaptability, appreciation for life's simple joys, ability to rebuild, sense of community, and perseverance through uncertainty. These qualities make you an amazing individual, and your story serves as a source of inspiration to us all. Recognizing and celebrating the extraordinary qualities that have emerged from your journey is essential.

Dreams and Aspirations:

As an individual, you have dreams and aspirations that are uniquely yours. You want to learn, work, and create a better life for yourself and your loved ones. Your circumstances may differ from those of others, but your hopes and desires remain unaltered. You see, being a refugee does not change the fundamental human longing for a better future.

When you, as a refugee, find yourself in unfamiliar and often challenging surroundings, it can be easy for others to overlook the common thread of humanity that binds everyone, including you. People may see the label of "refugee" before they see the person, but it is crucial to remember that behind that label lies an individual with their own set of dreams, passions, and goals.

Just like anyone else, you have a thirst for knowledge and a desire to learn. Education is a powerful tool that can empower you to shape your destiny, regardless of where you come from or where you find yourself. You may have left your home country due to conflict, persecution, or other dire circumstances, but that doesn't diminish your yearning for knowledge. You seek to understand the world, acquire new skills, and broaden your horizons.

Work is not just a means of financial support; it's a source of self-esteem and personal fulfillment. Just like anyone else, you desire the opportunity to contribute to society, to make a meaningful impact, and to support your family. Work provides a sense of purpose and accomplishment, and being a refugee does not diminish your drive to pursue your professional goals. You aspire to be self-reliant, to use your skills and talents, and to contribute to the communities that have offered you refuge.

The desire to make a better life for yourself and your family is a universal aspiration. As a refugee, you have faced upheaval and uncertainty, and the future may appear daunting. However, your commitment to improving your circumstances remains steadfast. You envision a life free from the turmoil and danger that led you to seek refuge. You dream of providing a stable and secure environment for your loved ones where they can grow, learn, and thrive.

The label of "refugee" should not obscure the fact that you, like anyone else, have an unquenchable thirst for a better life. Challenges and obstacles may have marked your journey, but your determination to rise above these difficulties is no different from the resolve of individuals who have not experienced displacement. You have an inherent resilience that propels you forward.

Your refugee status does not limit your dreams and aspirations. They are rather your strength and willingness to look ahead even though you seem to be forgotten from the rest of the world. You are not defined solely by your past or the circumstances that forced you to leave your homeland. Instead, you are defined by your vision for the future and your unwavering commitment to making it a reality.

As you navigate the complex path of resettlement and adaptation in a new environment, it's crucial to recognize the value of your dreams and aspirations. They are not mere fantasies; they are the driving force behind your resilience and determination. They serve as a guiding light, inspiring you to overcome the obstacles that stand in your way.

It's also important for society at large to acknowledge that refugees, like all individuals, have these dreams and aspirations. The label of "refugee" does not diminish their humanity or their potential. Empathy and understanding can help bridge the gap between refugees and their host communities, fostering a sense of belonging and unity.

Refugees share the same dreams and aspirations as anyone else. You want to learn, work, and create a better life for yourself and your family. Your refugee status may have added complexity to your journey, but it has not altered the fundamental essence of your hopes and desires. Your resilience and determination to pursue a brighter future serve as a reminder of the unbreakable spirit of your willingness to go above and beyond. It's essential to recognize and support these aspirations for the individuals who hold them and the societies that welcome them. After all, through understanding and collaboration, we can collectively work towards a world where every individual, regardless of their background, can achieve their dreams and aspirations.

Contributions to Society: Forced to leave their homes and everything familiar, refugees embark on a journey into the unknown, seeking safety, stability, and a chance to rebuild their lives. It is remarkable that, in the face of adversity, many refugees make significant contributions to their new communities. They become doctors, teachers, artists, and much more. Their experiences often make them more compassionate and understanding. Let us explore the inspiring stories of refugees who, much like you, have overcome the odds, demonstrated unwavering determination, and ultimately enriched the societies they now call home.

Imagine, for a moment, that you are a refugee. You've left behind your homeland, a place where memories and traditions were deeply ingrained, seeking refuge in a foreign land. The journey is perilous, fraught with uncertainty, and marked by countless challenges. The first step is to escape the immediate dangers that have forced you to flee—war, persecution, or environmental catastrophes. You find yourself in a foreign land, where you must navigate a complex web of laws, cultures, and languages. The first few months are undeniably challenging. You may feel like a stranger in a strange land, disconnected from everything familiar.

However, in your journey as a refugee, you discover something remarkable—resilience. This is a resilience born of necessity, of the need to adapt to a new environment and to provide a better future for yourself and your family. It is this resilience that drives many refugees to make significant contributions to their new communities.

One of the most striking ways refugees impact their host communities is through their professional contributions. Imagine that you, as a refugee, find yourself in a country that has granted you asylum. You don't know the language, you're not familiar with the local customs, and you lack the network many people take for granted in their home countries. Despite these challenges, refugees often embark on educational journeys that lead to impressive careers.

For example, as a refugee, you might decide to pursue a career in medicine. The desire to heal, to alleviate suffering, and to contribute positively to your new community motivates you. With immense determination, you navigate the complexities of medical school, working tirelessly to overcome language barriers and cultural differences. You find mentors and colleagues who appreciate your unique perspective, and you become a compassionate and skilled doctor, saving lives in your new homeland.

Similarly, consider the possibility of becoming a teacher. Education is a cornerstone of any society, and you recognize the importance of passing on knowledge and values to the next generation. So, you pursue a degree in education with the intent of empowering young minds to shape the future. Your experiences as a refugee instill in you a deep sense of empathy, enabling you to connect with students from diverse backgrounds. You become a beloved teacher, leaving an indelible mark on the lives of your students.

Another path you might choose as a refugee is that of an artist. Creativity often thrives in the face of adversity. As you grapple with the memories of your homeland and the experiences of your journey, you channel your emotions and experiences into your art. Your work bridges your past and present, a fact to human capacity for resilience and expression. Your art touches the hearts of your new community, fostering understanding and empathy.

Beyond these individual success stories, the collective contributions of refugees significantly impact the socioeconomic fabric of their new communities. As you, the refugee, establish yourself professionally, you also contribute to the economic development of your host country. You pay taxes, create jobs, and stimulate economic growth. This is not just about benefiting your own life; it's about contributing to the prosperity and well-being of the society that welcomed you.

Your journey as a refugee also shapes your worldview in profound ways. The experiences of loss, displacement, and adaptation imbue you with a deep sense of empathy and understanding. You know what it's like to be a stranger in a foreign land, to face prejudice, and to yearn for acceptance. This firsthand experience of being an outsider compels you to reach out to others who are marginalized or disadvantaged.

In your new community, you might become an advocate for refugees and other marginalized groups, just like the writer and author of this book. You share your story, shedding light on the challenges faced by refugees and working to dispel myths and stereotypes. Your advocacy helps create a more inclusive and compassionate society. You are not only a beneficiary of empathy but also a provider of it.

Furthermore, you might become involved in community-building initiatives, fostering bonds between the native population and refugees. These connections strengthen the social fabric, contributing to a more harmonious coexistence. Refugees are bridges between different worlds, a living power of resilience and hope for the unknowns.

The impact of refugees is not limited to their host countries. On a global scale, the contributions of refugees enrich the diversity and cultural tapestry of our interconnected world. As a refugee, you bring a piece of your culture with you, sharing it with your new community. This cultural exchange deepens understanding and appreciation for the richness of human diversity. The fusion of traditions, cuisines, and art forms creates a more vibrant and dynamic global society.

Consider the culinary arts, for example. As a refugee, you might introduce the flavours of your homeland to your new community. Your traditional dishes become a local favourite, celebrated by both refugees and natives. Food becomes a unifying force, transcending cultural boundaries and bringing people together.

In the realm of the arts, your unique perspective as a refugee informs your creative expression. You might collaborate with local artists, blending your experiences with their insights to produce works that resonate with a global audience. Art, music, and literature created by refugees often carry profound messages of resilience, hope, and the universality of the human experience. Refugee's path has the potential to inspire and enrich the societies they become part of.

As a refugee, you, too, have the power to overcome adversity, build a new life, and make significant contributions to your new community. Whether you become a doctor, a teacher, an artist, or an advocate, your experiences as a refugee instill in you a deep sense of empathy and understanding, qualities that bridge divides and foster a more compassionate society. The resilience and contributions of refugees are not only remarkable but also essential to building a more inclusive and harmonious world. By embracing and supporting refugees, societies not only provide a lifeline to those in need but also welcome individuals who have the potential to shape a brighter future for all.

Diversity and Culture: When refugees arrive in a new land, they carry with them the weight of their past and the wealth of their cultures and traditions. It becomes evident that you, as an individual, play a significant role in embracing and benefiting from this diversity. The presence of refugees in your community can undeniably enrich your life and the lives of those around you, making the environment more vibrant and interesting. It is a remarkable opportunity to learn, grow, and broaden your horizons.

As you open your heart and mind to refugees and their cultures, you will discover that the infusion of diverse backgrounds results in a more vibrant community. When you welcome them, you are contributing to a tapestry of experiences that transcends borders. You have the power to transform your neighbourhood into a melting pot of traditions, languages, and customs. This diversity can breathe new life into the place you call home, making it a hub of learning and understanding.

Imagine the aroma of exotic spices wafting from the kitchen of your new Syrian neighbours, who have brought the flavours of Aleppo to your doorstep. By taking an interest in their culinary traditions, you can learn to cook delicious dishes you may have never encountered before. As you share meals and recipes, you not only satisfy your taste buds but also bridge cultural gaps. Your curiosity and willingness to engage with their culture can lead to authentic friendships and a deeper appreciation of the world's gastronomic diversity.

Again, consider the music that resonates through your neighbourhood when Congolese refugees bring their vibrant rhythms to the local scene. By attending their performances or inviting them to share their music, you can embark on a cultural journey that transcends language. The universal language of music can transcend barriers, enabling you to communicate with your new neighbours on a profound level. Their melodies and beats can add a new layer of richness to the soundscape of your community, making it a more melodious and harmonious place to live.

As you take an active interest in the traditions of refugees, you are participating in a continuous exchange of knowledge. The stories and experiences they carry are treasures waiting to be shared. Listening to the tales of their homeland, their struggles, and their dreams can be a source of inspiration. You, in the second person, are not just a passive observer; you ᴜecome a part of their stories, helping shape your community's future through shared experiences.

Learning from refugees can also be an enlightening experience. Whether it's discovering the intricate art of Afghan carpet-making or understanding the symbolic meanings behind Chinese calligraphy, you can acquire new skills and knowledge. The rich cultural tapestry they bring can serve as a classroom without walls, expanding your horizons and broadening your skills. You can engage in workshops and classes or simply engage in one-on-one exchanges to learn and grow.

Moreover, refugees can serve as a powerful reminder of the universality of human experiences. When you take the time to hear their stories, you realize that despite differences in culture and geography, we share common hopes, dreams, and challenges. This realization becomes personal and transformative. You see yourself as a bridge, connecting different worlds, and in doing so, you become more attuned to the shared humanity that unites us all. This awareness can lead to a deeper sense of empathy and compassion, making you a better, more understanding individual.

The presence of refugees in your community also adds a layer of dynamism that can invigorate your everyday life. Their cultural celebrations, festivals, and events can infuse your surroundings with energy and excitement. You can attend these gatherings not as a spectator but as an active participant. You can learn to dance the traditional dances, participate in local festivals, and engage in communal celebrations that reflect the diversity of the people around you. In doing so, you become an integral part of these festivities, enhancing your own sense of belonging and enjoyment.

Remember, you are uniquely positioned to bridge gaps and build connections. By learning about their cultures and traditions, you are better equipped to promote understanding among your fellow community members. You can be a catalyst for change, inspiring others to embrace diversity and fostering an atmosphere of acceptance and unity.

However, it's crucial to recognize that this transformation is not a one-sided process. Your own culture and traditions are also valuable and deserving of sharing. Opening your heart and home to refugees can create a reciprocal exchange of knowledge and experiences. Your own customs and way of life become a part of the cultural mosaic, enriching the lives of others. This two-way street of cultural exchange ultimately contributes to the vitality and vibrancy of your community.

You have the power to make a difference. By actively engaging with refugees and their rich cultures, you can create a more inclusive, vibrant, and interesting community. Your openness, curiosity, and willingness to learn from and share with refugees can lead to personal growth, lasting friendships, and a deep appreciation for the diverse tapestry that is woven when people from different backgrounds come together. Embracing refugees is not just a gift to them but a gift to yourself and your entire community, making it a place where richness and diversity thrive, resulting in a more vibrant and interesting life for everyone involved.

Family and Relationships: You, as an individual, can readily relate to the fact that despite the upheaval and challenges a refugee may face, their capacity for love and forming deep connections remains unchanged. The experiences of displacement may have reshaped their external circumstances, but the core of who they are, and who you are, as a compassionate and relational being, remains unaltered.

Like you, refugees maintain a profound love for their family and friends. The ties that bind us to our loved ones are resilient and enduring. These relationships are not tethered to a specific location or circumstance. In the face of adversity, the love for family and friends often grows stronger, providing comfort and resilience. Just as you cherish the presence and support of your loved ones, refugees, too, hold their dear ones close to their hearts. They yearn for the well-being and safety of their families and friends, just as you do. This shared sentiment reminds us of the universality of love and the importance of human connections.

In addition, the ability to form strong bonds and relationships is an inherent human trait, unaltered by refugee status. Refugees, much like you, can create meaningful connections in their new environments. They bring with them not only their past experiences but also their potential for building new relationships. In the second person, you can understand that refugees are individuals with unique stories, talents, and dreams. Their refugee status does not limit their capacity to connect with others. As you engage with refugees, you have the opportunity to witness the resilience and strength of the human spirit, reinforcing the idea that connections can transcend borders and backgrounds.

Refugees often demonstrate incredible strength and adaptability, qualities that are essential for building relationships in new and sometimes unfamiliar settings. They can be your friends, coworkers, and neighbours, contributing to the diverse tapestry of your community. By acknowledging their ability to forge strong bonds, you, in the second person, can actively participate in fostering a more inclusive and welcoming environment.

You have the power to be a part of their journey and contribute to the creation of a supportive community. By recognizing the enduring love refugees have for their family and friends and their capacity to form deep relationships, you can play a crucial role in helping them rebuild their lives and find a sense of belonging in their new surroundings. Your empathy, understanding, and openness can make a significant difference in the lives of refugees, reinforcing the idea that despite the challenges they face, their ability to love and connect still remains at the center.

Hope and Resettlement: Refugees come with hope for a better future. They deserve a chance to rebuild their lives in a safe place, and their journey doesn't end with the label "refugee." It's just a phase in their life.

In simple terms, being called a refugee is like having a temporary label on your shirt. It might say "refugee," but underneath, you're still the same person with your unique personality, talents, and dreams. That label doesn't determine your future, and it doesn't make you any less valuable.

It's important to remember that we all face challenges in life, but how we overcome them defines us. Being a refugee is just one chapter in your story, not the whole book. You have the power to shape your future and create a life full of happiness, success, and fulfillment.

Don't let the name "refugee" define who you are. It's just a word used to describe a challenging situation you've been through. You are so much more than that label. You are strong, capable, and filled with potential. Embrace your dreams, keep moving forward, and remember that your past doesn't dictate your future.

CHAPTER IX

TRAVELLING TO NORTH AMERICA AND LIFE IN CANADA

The process of seeking resettlement assistance from the United Nations High Commissioner for Refugees (UNHCR) and relocating to Canada as a refugee is a complex and multi-step procedure that is both time-consuming and demanding. This process is essential for those who have been forced to flee their home countries due to persecution, violence, or other life-threatening circumstances and are seeking safety and a fresh start in a third country. The process involves various agencies and organizations.

I remember doing interviews with UNHCR officers, the goal of which was to determine my eligibility for resettlement. UNHCR Officers conducted a vulnerability assessment to determine whether my family and I faced specific risks. We successfully did well on the interviews. Our vulnerability was established and a referral to a Resettlement Country was made on our behalf.

Resettlement Eligibility:

Resettlement is generally offered to refugees who are unable to return to their home country due to a well-founded fear of persecution and for whom local integration into the host country is not possible, just like my situation. Eligibility criteria vary by country and may depend on factors such as family composition, medical conditions, security concerns, and other specific circumstances.

Interview and Selection:

We were deemed eligible for resettlement; we underwent an interview to determine our suitability for resettlement in a third country. This process often involves the government and its officials of the country that selected you. In my case, I was also interviewed by a representative from the Immigration Refugee Canada Citizenship (IRCC) Office in Zambia.

Security and Health Screening

After all the interviews, we underwent security and medical checks from Mehaba to Lusaka to ensure our health did not pose a security risk and were not carrying any contagious diseases. These screenings are a standard part of the resettlement process for refugees in many countries. However, on our seven-hour road journey to Lusaka for medical checks, something happened with the bus we were in.

As the driver steered the bus with an urgency born out of the fact that they were running late to pick us up, we found ourselves hurtling down the road toward Lusaka, the anticipation of the journey mixed with a palpable sense of anxiety. Little did we know that this voyage would soon take a terrifying turn.

In the midst of the journey, an event of sheer disbelief unfolded, endangering the happiness and well-being of the

26 passengers on board. With the bus hurtling along at a daunting speed of 120 kilometres per hour, the driver lost control, and the vehicle veered dangerously off the road, plunging into the wild tangle of bushes. It was a moment when time seemed to slow down, and fear gripped the hearts of everyone aboard.

However, in this perilous situation, our driver's true mettle shone through. His wealth of experience and quick thinking became our saving grace. With unwavering determination, he managed to keep a firm grip on the steering wheel, skillfully maneuvering the bus through the perilous terrain of trees and shrubbery.

Miraculously, the bus did not flip despite the high-speed impact with numerous trees along the way.

The skill, composure, and presence of mind displayed by the driver in that critical moment not only averted a potential disaster but also ensured the safety of all passengers. Skills of that driver showed an importance of having experienced professionals at the helm during unforeseen challenges. As the bus gradually stopped, we all breathed a sigh of relief, gratitude washing over us for the driver's remarkable expertise and ability to navigate a situation that could have ended in tragedy. Our journey continued, albeit with a renewed sense of appreciation for the fragility of life and the remarkable experience of IOM (International Organization for Migration) drivers.

Notification and Preparation

I vividly recall a particular Wednesday morning when I awoke, fully aware that it would be a significant day. As I got out of bed, I knew I had a busy day ahead of me as a Child and Youth Care Worker. My job required me to be in the field, roughly 15 kilometres away from my home.

With this in mind, I prepared myself for the day, ensuring I had everything I needed to carry out my duties effectively. After getting ready, I headed to my workplace, which was the Isibindi office in the UNHCR fence. There, my first task was to secure transportation to take me to the field. It was essential to make this journey because my responsibilities in the field were crucial for the children and youth I was working with.

While waiting for the transportation to become available, an unexpected and pivotal moment occurred. Staff members from the United Nations High Commissioner for Refugees (UNHCR) Solwezi office made an appearance at our office around 10:00 a.m. on Wednesday. They were there for a specific purpose, and the atmosphere in the office was charged with anticipation. They carried with them a list of names, a document of immense importance, which they promptly placed on the notice board for everyone to see.

Our family had been eagerly awaiting news about our resettlement, and the day had finally arrived when we received the long-anticipated notification. We had been diligently following the process, and to say that we were on tenterhooks would be an understatement. It was a moment filled with suspense and excitement, as we had been longing to learn the crucial details of our relocation to Canada.

As I was deeply engrossed in my work at the time, I was completely unaware of the life-changing news that was about to unfold. It was one of those busy days when the demands of the office had consumed my attention. However, fate had other plans, and the universe was determined to pull me out of my work-mode bubble.

In this pivotal moment, my close friends, who were clearly more in tune with the significance of the news, seized the opportunity to break through my oblivious state. With a sense of urgency and anticipation, they yanked me away from my desk, making it clear that something extraordinary was happening.

"Bazi, come quick!" they exclaimed, excitement coursing through their voices, "Your name is on the list for Canada!" These words hit me like a thunderbolt, and suddenly, the weight of their message began to sink in.

At first, I was in disbelief, my mind struggling to comprehend the magnitude of what I had just heard. It was an announcement that changed everything, and it was difficult to fathom the reality of such a life-altering event. Yet, my friends' persistence and insistence began to break through my disbelief.

Not willing to let me continue my work obliviously, one of my friends returned for a second time, pulling my hand off the table. With determination in his eyes, he made sure that there was no escaping the moment that had arrived. We hastily exited the office, and as we stepped outside, a wave of excitement engulfed us. It wasn't just my friends who had recognized the significance of the news; it seemed like the entire world had converged to witness this momentous occasion.

There, in a chorus of joy and congratulations, everyone around us began to shout, "Bazi, we have seen your family name!" It was a moment of pure jubilation, and the air was filled with the electrifying energy of new beginnings and the promise of a brighter future. The news had not only pulled me away from my busy work life but had also pulled us into a new chapter in our lives, a chapter that was written with dreams of resettlement and hope for a better life in Canada.

Pre-departure Orientation:

In the weeks leading up to our departure, we engaged in a series of comprehensive orientation sessions designed to equip us with the knowledge and tools needed to navigate our new life in Canada. These sessions were invaluable in helping us prepare for the exciting journey ahead and provided a roadmap for our integration into a new culture and society.

The orientation seminar was a treasure trove of information thoughtfully curated to address every aspect of life in Canada. One of the most illuminating segments of the seminar delved into the intricacies of Canadian culture. We were guided through the rich tapestry of customs, traditions, and values that form the heart and soul of this multicultural nation. Learning about the diverse festivals, the significance of Canadian holidays, and the nuances of everyday interactions helped us better understand the cultural mosaic we were about to become a part of. It was an eye-opening experience that fostered a profound appreciation for the cultural diversity that Canada proudly embraces.

In addition to cultural insights, the orientation also gave us a clear understanding of the legal requirements and obligations we would encounter upon arriving in Canada. We were guided through the immigration and visa processes, ensuring we had a firm grasp of the legal framework that would govern our status in the country. Understanding our rights and responsibilities was crucial to establishing a strong foundation for our new life in Canada, and these sessions ensured we were well-informed and prepared.

Furthermore, the seminar went beyond theoretical knowledge by offering practical guidance on accessing essential services. We learned how to navigate the Canadian healthcare system, find quality education for our children, and secure housing that met our needs. The knowledge imparted in these sessions empowered us to make informed decisions and seamlessly integrate into our new community.

These orientation sessions were a vital part of our pre-departure preparations, leaving us excited and well-prepared for the adventure that awaited us in Canada. They instilled in us a sense of confidence, a profound respect for Canadian culture, and the essential information needed to embark on this new chapter of our lives with enthusiasm and optimism.

Travel to Canada

The UNHCR, the United Nations High Commissioner for Refugees, embarked on the crucial first step in our resettlement journey by initiating our case. They carefully assessed our situation and eligibility, recognizing the need for a new beginning in a safe environment. The UNHCR laid the foundation for our hopeful future with compassion and dedication.

Subsequently, the International Organization for Migration (IOM) took over, serving as the invaluable guiding force that meticulously prepared us for our impending journey. They equipped us with the necessary information, resources, and support, ensuring that we were mentally, emotionally, and physically prepared for the challenges and opportunities ahead. Their expertise and care were instrumental in bolstering our confidence and readiness for what was to come.

In an inspiring display of humanitarianism and solidarity, the Canadian government played a pivotal role in facilitating our resettlement. They generously covered the cost of our flights, removing a significant barrier to our transition. Their financial support not only made our journey feasible but also highlighted their commitment to providing us with a fresh start in their country.

Throughout this intricate process, the UNHCR, IOM, and the Canadian Government worked in perfect harmony, ensuring seamless coordination and cooperation. Their collective efforts were a testament to the power of international cooperation and the dedication of individuals and organizations committed to improving the lives of refugees. Together, they transformed what could have been a daunting experience into a journey of hope, promise, and new beginnings.

In the days leading up to our departure, we received clear instructions that a bus, arranged by IOM dispatched from Lusaka, would soon arrive at Meheba Settlement to collect our family. As the day of our departure approached, excitement and apprehension filled our hearts. We knew what we had to do, as the details of the journey and what to pack had been thoroughly explained during our training sessions.

We woke up the morning we were set to leave before the sun had risen. It was a disorienting mix of emotions as we stood there trying to decide what to pack and what to leave behind. Despite receiving comprehensive guidance, choosing what would accompany us on our new journey was still a challenge. It felt as if every item held a piece of our past, and parting with them was not just about shedding possessions but memories and attachments, too.

As the bus drew nearer, the reality of our departure began to sink in. The weight of leaving behind friends, good neighbours, and the countless other people we had formed deep connections within Meheba Settlement was overwhelming. The bonds we had forged, the stories we had shared, and the support we had offered one another made leaving an emotional and bittersweet experience. Showcasing the profound impact communites and connection can have on our lives. We were embarking on a new chapter, but the fond memories and cherished relationships with Meheba would forever hold a special place in our hearts.

Before embarking on our journey to the airport, we were given a set of crucial documents neatly packed in a plastic bag, a bag I affectionately called the "White Magic Plastic Bag." This plastic bag prominently bore the abbreviation "IOM" on both sides, signifying its importance and our connection to the International Organization for Migration. We were given clear instructions to carry this bag in our hands and always keep it visible to the public, at least until we safely touched down in Canada.

Initially, I couldn't help but feel a bit self-conscious lugging this plastic bag around as we embarked on our long-haul flight. While I understood on an intellectual level that it had a significant purpose in our journey, the true value of this seemingly ordinary plastic bag only became clear when I encountered a moment of uncertainty and panic during a layover in Frankfurt, Germany.

As I navigated the bustling and complex Frankfurt Airport, I inadvertently ended up at an unfamiliar gate, disoriented and unsure of how to find my way back to my original point of entry. I was effectively lost in a foreign airport, overwhelmed by the sheer size and complexity of it all. In this moment of distress, the "White Magic Plastic Bag" revealed its true worth.

A stranger, a kind lady wearing a blue top, approached me. To my amazement, I noticed the IOM symbol on her clothing. She greeted me with a warm smile and inquired about my destination. I tried to save face by explaining that I had merely stepped out to stretch my legs and had lost my way back. She continued to ask me more crucial questions, such as my flight number, gate information, and departure time. To my chagrin, I had no answers to any of her inquiries, and it felt embarrassing to respond repeatedly with a helpless "I DON'T KNOW." It was as though I had only ever learned the phrase "I DON'T KNOW" in my entire life.

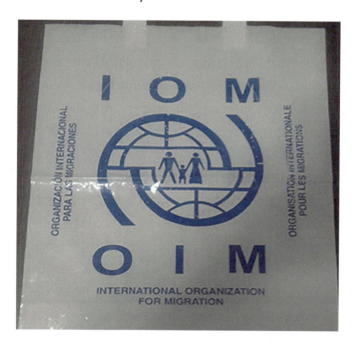

However, the stranger's friendly demeanour put me at ease. I mustered the courage to ask her why she had approached me so urgently. Her response left me both humbled and grateful. She said, "I noticed that IOM plastic bag in your hand, and I knew I could assist you if you needed help." It was then that the significance of the instructions given to me by the IOM agent in Zambia became clear. The purpose of carrying that plastic bag was not just symbolic; it was a lifeline, a beacon of support, and a tangible connection to assistance in unfamiliar and challenging situations.

At that moment, I realized that the "White Magic Plastic Bag" had been my ticket to safety and guidance when I needed it most. It was a universal symbol that transcended language barriers, connecting me to the network of people and support systems put in place to ensure my successful journey to Canada. Without that simple plastic bag, I might have remained lost, listening to stories about Canada on the radio instead of experiencing it firsthand. This experience underscored the power of seemingly ordinary objects and the importance of following instructions, even when their true significance might not be immediately apparent.

Arrival in Canada

When we arrived in Canada as permanent residents, we went through customs and immigration procedures to enter the country officially. Here's what to expect.

Arrival at the Port of Entry: You will do so at a designated Port of Entry (POE) when you arrive in Canada. This could be an international airport, a land border crossing, or a marine port. Make sure you have all the required documents, such as your Confirmation of Permanent Residence (COPR), a valid passport, and any other supporting documents.

Initial Customs Check: At the port of entry, you will first go through a customs check. You'll be asked about the goods you're bringing with you, and you may need to declare any items subject to customs duties or taxes.

Immigration and Documentation Check: After clearing customs, you will proceed to the immigration checkpoint. Here, an immigration officer will review your documents, including your COPR, travel documents, and any other relevant paperwork. Canadian Immigration Officer will confirm your status.

Biometrics and Photos: If you haven't already done so, you may be required to provide biometrics (fingerprints and a photo). For my family and I, we did everything in Zambia.

Completing the Confirmation of Permanent Residence (COPR): If your documents are in order and you meet all the requirements, the immigration officer will complete your COPR, which includes an official stamp. This confirms your status as a permanent resident of Canada.

Welcome to Canada Kit: You may receive a "Welcome to Canada" kit, which contains important information about your rights and responsibilities as a permanent resident, as well as information about living in Canada. This kit also includes contact information for various government agencies and organizations that can assist you.

Assistance from Resettlement Organizations: In some cases, resettlement organizations or volunteers may be present to provide additional support and information. They can help you with questions and assist with your initial settlement needs, such as finding accommodation, opening a bank account, and understanding local services. In my family's case, we were thoroughly assisted with Social catholic services.

Health Screening: You may undergo a health screening depending on your circumstances and the specific port of entry. In the context of a global pandemic, there might be additional health and safety measures in place.

Social Insurance Number (SIN): If you don't already have one, you can also apply for a Social Insurance Number (SIN) at the port of entry. A SIN is necessary for various government services, including employment and benefits.

It's important to ensure you have all the necessary documentation and meet the requirements for entry into Canada as a permanent resident. The process may vary slightly depending on your specific port of entry and the current immigration regulations, so it's a good idea to check the most up-to-date information on the official website of the Government of Canada or consult with immigration authorities for any changes or specific requirements.

Upon arriving in Canada, I was fortunate to benefit from a comprehensive resettlement assistance program encompassing various essential components, such as language training, dedicated employment support, and a wide range of invaluable social services. This holistic support was thoughtfully designed to cater to the unique circumstances and needs of newcomers like me, ensuring that I had the necessary resources and guidance to integrate into Canadian society successfully. The specific nature, extent, and duration of this assistance were meticulously adapted to my situation, allowing me to embark on my journey of resettlement with confidence and a strong support network by my side.

Refugee Resettlement:

In the heart of the Northern Hemisphere lies a nation known for its breathtaking landscapes and its deep commitment to compassion and inclusivity. Canada, a country with a rich history of resettling refugees, stands as a ray of hope for those seeking safety from the storms of conflict, persecution, and humanitarian crises.

At the forefront of Canada's humanitarian efforts is its active participation in international refugee resettlement programs. The country extends its arms wide, welcoming refugees from various corners of the globe, embodying a tradition deeply ingrained in its ethos. This commitment is underpinned by a robust legal framework, including the Refugee and Immigration Protection Acts, designed to protect and uphold the rights of those seeking refuge on Canadian soil.

Beyond the legal realm, Canada offers an array of immigration programs, each designed to cater to the diverse needs of individuals yearning for a new beginning. The Express Entry system, comprising the Federal Skilled Worker Program, the Canadian Experience Class, and the Federal Skilled Trades Program, is a proof to Canada's dedication to providing opportunities for those with different skill sets. Provincial nominee programs further tailor immigration pathways, aligning with specific labour market and economic needs.

Family reunification is a cornerstone of Canadian immigration policy. The emphasis on reuniting families underscores the country's commitment to preserving the bonds that tie us together. Canadian citizens and permanent residents can sponsor immediate family members, creating a haven where loved ones can rebuild their lives together.

Canada's allure extends beyond humanitarian grounds. The vast landscape of economic opportunities beckons immigrants, offering job prospects, access to quality education, and avenues for entrepreneurship. The country boasts a robust and diverse economy, encouraging newcomers to contribute to its growth and prosperity.

In the process of integration, immigrants and refugees find solace in Canada's extensive social services and support systems. From healthcare to education, language training to settlement programs, a safety net is woven to ease the transition into Canadian society.

Canada's strength lies in its multicultural fabric. The nation embraces people from all walks of life and celebrates diversity and inclusivity. The government actively champions these values, fostering a welcoming environment that reverberates in the multicultural communities thriving in Canadian cities.

As a global player in humanitarian initiatives, Canada extends its hand beyond its borders, providing financial support and resources to refugees and displaced populations worldwide. The nation's commitment to alleviating global suffering underscores its belief in the interconnectedness of humanity.

Crucially, this welcoming stance finds resonance within the Canadian public. A positive attitude toward refugees and immigrants prevails, with community organizations and volunteers actively contributing to the integration efforts of newcomers. The collective embrace of diversity transforms Canada into a sought-after destination for those yearning to build anew in a society that values every individual's contribution.

LIVING IN WINTER COUNTRY

SYMBOLIZING THE REFUGEE EXPERIENCE: CONTRASTING EDMONTON'S CLIMATE WITH ZAMBIA'S

The world has diverse climates, landscapes, and environments, each with its unique charm and challenges. Edmonton, a city nestled in the heart of Canada, stands in stark contrast to Zambia's lush, tropical or subtropical climate. While these weather disparities may seem unrelated, they can be a poignant metaphor for the feelings experienced by refugees when they arrive in a foreign land. For refugees who have left behind the familiarity of their homeland to seek refuge in Edmonton, the significant shift in weather is more than just a meteorological contrast; it symbolizes a profound transformation in their lives.

Let's look into the reasons behind Edmonton's unique climate and explore how this climate, distinct from Zambia's, mirrors the emotional journey of refugees arriving in a foreign land.

Understanding Edmonton's Climate

Edmonton, the capital city of Alberta, Canada, boasts a subarctic climate. It experiences four distinct seasons: spring, summer, fall, and winter. Such a climate, characterized by temperature extremes, can be vastly different from the more stable, tropical or subtropical conditions in Zambia.

Winter in Edmonton is long and harsh, with frigid temperatures that can plummet well below freezing. Snowfall is abundant, and the cityscape is often blanketed in white, giving it a serene, almost magical appearance. Spring brings a welcome thaw as the snow gradually melts and reveals the promise of new life. Summers in Edmonton are warm and pleasant, with temperatures often reaching a comfortable range, making it a popular time for outdoor activities. Autumn paints the city with a riot of colours as the leaves on the deciduous trees turn various shades of red, yellow, and orange before eventually falling to the ground.

Edmonton's climate thus symbolizes a cycle of change and transformation, with each season representing a distinct phase. This climate stands in stark contrast to the consistent warmth and humidity I experienced in Zambia, where tropical or subtropical conditions prevailed year-round. Much like the refugee experience, the city's climate embodies the idea of adaptation, resilience, and the inevitability of change.

The Refugee Experience

When I consider the emotions and experiences of refugees who leave their homeland, I find that these, too, go through a cycle of change and transformation, similar to the changing seasons of Edmonton. Refugees are often forced to flee their countries due to war, persecution, or natural disasters. We leave behind our homes, communities, and sometimes even our families, embarking on a perilous journey in search of safety and a better life.

The initial stage of my refugee journey can be almost the same as Edmonton's harsh winter. It is a time of great uncertainty, fear, and discomfort. Refugees face numerous challenges, from the perilous journey itself to the legal and logistical hurdles of seeking asylum in a new country. This is a time of adaptation and resilience, as we must quickly learn to navigate unfamiliar terrain and customs. The metaphorical "snow" of this winter stage may be the emotional weight of leaving our homeland, the language barriers, and the anxiety of an uncertain future.

Just as spring arrives in Edmonton, the refugee experience often brings hope. Refugees may find safety, shelter, and a supportive community in our host country, which can be likened to the thawing of winter's chill. We begin to rebuild our lives, often assisted by local organizations and governments, and we may find opportunities for education, employment, and integration into the local culture.

Summer in Edmonton represents a time of relative stability and warmth, much like the period when refugees find their footing in the host country. During this phase, they may establish themselves in their new community, make friends, and contribute to the local economy and society. It's a time of growth and personal development.

Autumn's arrival in Edmonton signifies the transformation and growth refugees undergo as they become more deeply rooted in their host country. They may reflect on their journey, their past, and their future. This phase is a reminder that their experiences, both the challenges and the victories, have coloured their identity and enriched their lives. Much like the changing leaves in autumn, the refugee's story has become a tapestry of vibrant experiences and memories.

Edmonton's climate, with its distinctive seasons, can serve as a metaphor for the emotional journey of refugees who arrive in this city from regions like Zambia, where climates are relatively stable and unchanging. The transition from Zambia's tropical or subtropical climate to Edmonton's subarctic climate can be seen as an allegory for the profound transformation and adaptation that refugees undergo.

Just as Edmonton's climate cycles through the seasons, the refugee experience encompasses stages of initial turmoil, adaptation, hope, stability, and personal growth. The challenges and triumphs of the refugee journey are echoed in the changing landscapes and weather patterns of Edmonton. Together, they remind us of the human capacity for resilience and adaptation, no matter how different the climate may be from what we once knew. In both cases, the beauty and richness of the experience lie in embracing change and finding strength in transformation.

Adapting to Edmonton's Harsh Weather: A Journey of Resilience

When I first arrived in Edmonton, Alberta, I was immediately confronted with the reality of its harsh weather. The cold, unforgiving winters and the unpredictable climate were a stark contrast to the milder weather I had been accustomed to. Adapting to Edmonton's climate was not a choice but a necessity. I undertook this transformative journey, focusing on three key aspects: necessity, embracing the challenge, and pursuing a normal life.

The first and most fundamental factor that drove me to adapt to Edmonton's harsh weather was necessity. I had relocated to this city for various reasons, including pursuing my education and, subsequently, my career. I had no other option but to face the elements head-on. The weather can be unforgiving in Edmonton, with winters stretching on forever and temperatures plummeting well below freezing. I needed to learn to adapt, not just for my well-being but for achieving my goals.

My journey began with the realization that there was no escape from the weather. Unlike milder climates where I had previously lived, I couldn't simply wait for the weather to improve. In Edmonton, the winter season was a formidable force that arrived with determination and stayed for a significant part of the year. I had to equip myself with the right clothing, which meant investing in quality winter gear. From heavy coats to insulated boots and warm gloves, I gradually built a wardrobe that would allow me to venture outdoors comfortably, even in the coldest of temperatures.

Learning to love the weather, or at least pretend to, was another crucial aspect of my adaptation. While I might not have genuinely fallen in love with Edmonton's cold and snowy winters, maintaining a positive attitude was essential. I adopted the local saying, "There's no such thing as bad weather, only bad clothing." This phrase encapsulated the mindset of many Edmontonians who embraced the winter as an integral part of their lives. It encouraged me to see the beauty in a crisp, snowy morning or to appreciate the cozy feeling of sitting by a warm fire on a cold winter night. By changing my perspective and focusing on the positive aspects of the weather, I was better equipped to cope with its challenges.

Furthermore, I observed the local population and learned from their habits and practices. Edmontonians had developed a unique relationship with their climate, and I realized I needed to do the same. Ice skating, skiing, and even winter festivals were all a part of life in Edmonton, and I decided to participate in these activities. Engaging in these winter pastimes not only helped me embrace the season but also enabled me to connect with the local community. During these experiences, I discovered the warmth of Edmontonians, who were always ready to offer advice and support to newcomers like me.

My pursuit of education and the desire to build meaningful connections was the most compelling motivation to adapt to Edmonton's harsh weather. I had enrolled in a College Named NorQuest College in Edmonton, and attending classes was a non-negotiable part of my journey. Missing classes due to bad weather was not an option. This motivation pushed me to brave the elements, trudging through snowdrifts and enduring icy winds to attend classes. Education was my passport to a better future, and I was determined not to let the weather be a hindrance.

Making friends and building meaningful connections in a new city were equally important to me. Adapting to the local culture and climate was key to forging these relationships. I began by engaging in conversations with my fellow students at Norquest College, many of whom were also newcomers to Edmonton. We shared our experiences, exchanged tips for surviving the winter, and formed a tight-knit support group. These connections helped us cope with the challenges of the climate and provided a sense of belonging.

In addition to my Norquest College peers, I also sought to be part of the wider community. Edmontonians are known for their friendliness and willingness to help newcomers. I attended local events and joined community groups, which allowed me to adapt to the weather and enriched my life with diverse experiences. Whether participating in a community snowshoeing event or volunteering at a winter festival, I found that embracing the local culture and climate was the key to forming lasting connections.

It wasn't long before I began to appreciate the beauty of Edmonton's winters. The pristine white snow covering the landscape, the glistening icicles hanging from trees, and the crisp, fresh air inspired me. I started to take up winter photography as a hobby, capturing the serene beauty of the city in its frozen splendour. Through my lens, I discovered a new perspective on the harsh weather, one that allowed me to see the artistic side of winter.

Trust me when I say adapting to Edmonton's harsh weather was a transformative journey encompassing necessity, embracing the challenge, and pursuing a normal life. I learned that resilience was the key to thriving in a challenging environment. Necessity forced me to face the weather head-on, and I equipped myself with the right clothing and gear. Embracing the challenge required changing my perspective and adopting a positive attitude toward the weather, ultimately allowing me to participate in winter activities and engage with the local community. Pursuing a normal life, including education and meaningful connections, was my driving force, motivating me to endure the harshest winters.

Edmonton's climate, once seen as a monster, became a formidable but ultimately conquerable adversary. In the end, I adapted to the harsh weather and found beauty and fulfillment in the unique experiences it offered. With their challenges and charm, Edmonton's winters became an integral part of my life, shaping me into a more resilient and adaptable individual.

YOU ARE NOT ALONE; YOU ARE NOT FORGOTTEN—EDMONTON TRANSIT SYSTEM

Using the Buses

Embracing the comprehensive bus system and taking the time to familiarize oneself with Edmonton's intricate web of addresses and routes is an indispensable journey for those seeking to extract the utmost enjoyment from their stay in this dynamic and bustling city. Opting for the convenience and accessibility of public transportation isn't just a practical choice; it's a commitment to sustainability and an eco-conscious mode of travel that ultimately benefits not only the traveller but also the environment.

Relying on the city's public transit network opens the door to a world of possibilities, providing an efficient, cost-effective, and hassle-free means of navigating the urban landscape. With Edmonton's well-maintained and extensive bus system at your disposal, you can effortlessly traverse the city's diverse neighbourhoods, each offering its unique charm and character. From the vibrant artsy districts to the serene residential areas, the bus system ensures you can effortlessly hop from one locale to another, immersing yourself in the rich tapestry of Edmonton's culture and lifestyle.

Public transportation offers a window into the heart of Edmonton's cultural hubs and various attractions. Whether you're looking to explore the renowned galleries, museums, theatres, or the city's thriving culinary scene, the bus system is a reliable conduit to all these experiences. It frees you from the constraints of parking woes and traffic hassles, granting you the precious gift of time to immerse yourself fully in the city's myriad cultural offerings.

Public transportation ensures you remain connected to the pulse of the city's ever-evolving events and activities. Be it a festival in the heart of downtown, a sports game at a stadium, or a live concert at a buzzing entertainment venue, the bus system positions you just a ride away from the action. It eliminates the need for costly parking fees and traffic-induced stress, allowing you to relish every moment of your urban adventure.

Embracing Edmonton's bus system is akin to unlocking the key to the city's treasures. It simplifies your exploration of its diverse neighbourhoods and cultural wonders and aligns your journey with the values of sustainability and eco-consciousness.

With public transportation, you are not just a visitor but an active participant in Edmonton's dynamic, vibrant, and ever-evolving landscape.

Benefits of Using Public Buses in Edmonton

Using buses in Edmonton offers several benefits for both residents and the community. Some of the key advantages I enjoy using buses in Edmonton daily include:

Environmental Benefits:

Reduced greenhouse gas emissions: Buses are generally more fuel-efficient and produce fewer emissions per passenger than individual cars, helping reduce air pollution and combat climate change.

Improved air quality: Fewer cars on the road means reduced air pollution, which can have a positive impact on public health.

Cost Savings: Buses are typically more cost-effective than owning and maintaining a personal vehicle, as they eliminate fuel, insurance, and maintenance expenses.

Fare options: Edmonton often offers a variety of fare options, including discounted passes for students and seniors, making public transit more affordable.

Reduced Traffic Congestion: Buses help reduce the number of private vehicles on the road, alleviating traffic congestion and making commuting more efficient.

Dedicated bus lanes: Many cities, including Edmonton, have implemented dedicated bus lanes and transit priority measures to improve bus speed and reliability.

Accessibility:

Inclusive transportation: Buses are designed to be accessible for people with disabilities, including wheelchair ramps and priority seating.

Extensive network: Edmonton's bus system typically covers a wide area, making it easier for residents to access various parts of the city.

Safety:

Lower accident rates: Public transportation is generally safer than driving a personal vehicle, as professional drivers are trained to navigate traffic and handle various situations.

Reduced drunk driving: Public transit provides a safe and convenient alternative to drinking and driving, which can help reduce accidents and fatalities.

Social Benefits:

Enhanced community connections: Buses connect people to their workplaces, schools, and recreational activities, fostering a sense of community.

Reduced social isolation: Public transportation can help individuals without access to private vehicles maintain social connections and access essential services.

Reduced Infrastructure Costs:

Reduced road maintenance: Fewer private vehicles on the road can lower maintenance and repair costs for the city's road infrastructure.

Savings on parking infrastructure: Reducing the need for extensive parking facilities can free up land for other uses and reduce costs.

Navigating a New World: The Challenge of Learning Edmonton's Streets and Avenues as a Refugee

For refugees escaping conflict, persecution, or economic hardship, the journey to a new land brings both hope and challenges. One of the most daunting challenges refugees face is adapting to their new environment, and a crucial aspect of this adaptation is learning the layout of the city where they have found refuge. Understanding its streets and avenues can be particularly challenging in the case of Edmonton, Alberta, Canada, given its vast expanse and unique addressing system.

Edmonton's Geographical Landscape

Edmonton, Alberta's capital city, is known for its stunning natural surroundings, characterized by the North Saskatchewan River Valley, which offers a unique blend of urban and natural environments. The city is divided into several neighbourhoods and communities, each with its own distinct characteristics and, more importantly, its own network of streets and avenues.

Edmonton's Addressing System

Edmonton's addressing system is another layer of complexity for newcomers. Edmonton uses a quadrant-based system, unlike the conventional grid system in many North American cities. The city is divided into four quadrants: Northwest (NW), Northeast (NE), Southwest (SW), and Southeast (SE). Each quadrant is bisected by Jasper Avenue (101 Avenue) and 101

Street, which serves as the city's baseline for street numbering. This means street addresses increase numerically as you move away from Jasper Avenue, while avenues increase numerically as you move away from 101 Street. The combination of street number and avenue number is used to pinpoint a specific location within the city.

For instance, an address such as "105(00) 82 Avenue NW" means the location is on 105th Street and 82nd Avenue in the Northwest quadrant. This unique addressing system is often perplexing for newcomers accustomed to more straightforward street grids, where streets are numbered in a predictable pattern.

Challenges for Refugees to Know the Addresses.

I remember when I arrived in Edmonton, I faced numerous challenges, and adapting to the city's streets and avenues was just one of them. These challenges were profound and hindered my integration and overall well-being. Below are some of the difficulties I encountered when I learned about Edmonton's streets and avenues:

Language Barrier: Many refugees like me arrive with limited or no knowledge of English or French, Canada's official languages. Navigating the city and understanding street signs can be exceptionally challenging when language is a barrier. Reading and understanding road signs and maps are essential for safely and efficiently getting around.

Unfamiliar Addressing System: The quadrant-based addressing system in Edmonton is notably different from the systems in their home countries. It can be confusing for newcomers, making it challenging to determine their location or the location of a specific address.

Lack of Local Knowledge: I lacked local knowledge about Edmonton's neighbourhoods, and landmarks. This lack of familiarity made judging distances, planning routes, and feeling comfortable in my new surroundings difficult.

Limited Resources: Many refugees just like me arrive in Edmonton with limited financial resources. This can restrict our ability to access smartphones, GPS devices, or even public transportation, which could assist us in navigating the city.

Cultural Isolation: The feeling of cultural isolation can be overwhelming, as refugees may find it challenging to connect with locals and establish social networks. Navigating the streets is closely linked to cultural integration and building a sense of belonging.

Support Systems for Newcomers

Despite these challenges, Edmontonians offered me a range of support systems and resources to help me adapt to the city's streets and avenues:

Settlement Agencies: Several settlement agencies in Edmonton provided support for me when I came. These agencies offer orientation sessions, language classes, and information on local services. They can also help you understand the addressing system and navigate the city more effectively.

Community Organizations: Various community organizations and cultural centers provide resources and support for newcomers. They often organize events and activities to help refugees connect with the local community, which can assist in gaining a better understanding of the city's layout.

Language Classes: Learning English or French is essential for refugees to overcome language barriers. Edmonton offers a range of language classes and programs to facilitate this process, enabling newcomers to read road signs and communicate effectively.

Local Guides and Mentorship Programs: Some organizations in Edmonton run mentorship programs where newcomers are paired with local volunteers. These mentors can help refugees navigate the city, explain the addressing system, and introduce them to the local culture and customs.

Transportation Resources: Edmonton's public transportation system plays a vital role in helping newcomers travel throughout the city. Information on routes and schedules is readily available, making it easier for refugees to access essential services and employment opportunities.

The Impact of Learning Edmonton's Streets and Avenues

The ability to navigate a city's streets and avenues is more than just a matter of convenience; it directly impacts the lives and well-being of refugees in several ways:

Safety: Understanding the city's streets and avenues is crucial for personal safety. Refugees who confidently navigate their surroundings are less likely to find themselves in unsafe or unfamiliar areas.

Employment Opportunities: Knowing how to reach potential job locations is essential for refugees seeking employment. Navigational skills can significantly impact their ability to attend interviews and secure jobs.

Access to Services: Refugees need access to various services, including healthcare, education, and government offices. Knowing the streets and avenues is essential for accessing these services and integrating into the local community.

Cultural Integration: Refugees who feel confident about moving around the city are more likely to explore their new surroundings, engage in community activities, and develop a sense of belonging.

Mental Well-being: The ability to navigate the city reduces stress and anxiety for refugees. It empowers them to be more independent and self-reliant, positively affecting their mental health.

Learning the streets and avenues of Edmonton is a crucial step for refugees to adapt to their new environment. The city's unique quadrant-based addressing system, combined with language barriers and a lack of local knowledge, can create significant challenges. However, Edmonton offers numerous resources and support systems to help refugees like me overcome these challenges and build a better life in their new homes.

Navigating the city's streets and avenues is not just a practical skill; it's a gateway to safety, employment, access to services, cultural integration, and overall well-being. As refugees become more familiar with their surroundings, they not only find their way around Edmonton but also find their place in the city's diverse and welcoming community. Today, I have overcome the initial struggles and am now fully familiar with our addresses and venues in Edmonton.

CHAPTER X

CULTURAL DIVERSITY: EDMONTON'S RICH AND DIVERSE CULTURE

Edmonton, the capital city of Alberta, Canada, is a vibrant and diverse urban center known for its rich culture. The city's history reflects the multiple waves of immigration that have contributed to its dynamic cultural mosaic. Edmonton's diverse culture encompasses many traditions, languages, and artistic expressions, making it a fascinating place to explore and appreciate.

Historical Foundations of Cultural Diversity

Edmonton's cultural diversity has deep historical roots and can be traced back to its indigenous heritage and early European settlers. The region's Indigenous peoples, including Cree, Dene, Blackfoot, and Métis, have lived in the area for millennia. Their languages, traditions, and art forms have contributed significantly to the cultural landscape. Edmonton's very name is derived from the Cree word "Amiskwaciy" which means "Beaver Hills," reflecting the Indigenous presence and significance of the area's natural resources.

In the late 18th century, European explorers and fur traders, predominantly from France and Britain, began to settle in the region, further enriching the cultural milieu. The fur trade brought together indigenous peoples and European settlers and played a crucial role in shaping Edmonton's cultural diversity. It provides a platform for the exchange of languages, knowledge, and traditions between these two distinct groups, fostering a unique blend of Indigenous and European influences.

As Edmonton developed into an established city in the late 19th and early 20th centuries, additional waves of immigration were added to its cultural fabric. European, Chinese, Ukrainian, and other communities flocked to the city for economic opportunities and new life. This influx of diverse cultures has brought to the city a wide range of languages, cuisines, and artistic expressions, further enhancing its multicultural character.

Today, Edmonton continues to be a melting pot of culture, with a broad spectrum of communities shaping its cultural landscape. The city is home to numerous cultural and ethnic communities, each contributing to the richness of Edmonton's diverse culture. Some prominent communities include the following.

Indigenous Communities: Edmonton remains in traditional territory, and indigenous cultures continue to be a fundamental part of the city's identity. Various Indigenous communities contribute to the local culture through their languages, art, and ceremonies, preserving their heritage while sharing it with others.

Ukrainian Community: Edmonton is home to one of the largest Ukrainian communities in Canada. This community has significantly contributed to the city's cultural scene through events such as the Ukrainian Festival and vibrant Ukrainian dance and music traditions.

Chinese Community: The Chinese community in Edmonton has a strong presence, offering a rich array of cuisines and cultural festivals. The Chinese New Year celebration is a significant event in the city that attracts residents and visitors alike.

South Asian Community: Edmonton's South Asian community, predominantly of Indian and Pakistani descent, has enriched the city with diverse culinary offerings, cultural festivals, and traditional dance and music.

African and Caribbean Communities: These communities have brought distinctive traditions and vibrant music and dance styles to the city. Festivals celebrating African and Caribbean cultures provide a glimpse of their rich heritage.

European Communities: The European presence in Edmonton remains strong, with various communities such as German, Italian, and Scottish maintaining their cultural traditions through cultural festivals and clubs.

The city exemplifies a remarkable sense of inclusivity and open-mindedness, extending a warm and heartfelt welcome to everyone, irrespective of their beliefs, sexuality, or diverse backgrounds. It stands as a beacon of tolerance and acceptance where people from all walks of life can find a place to belong and thrive. This city fosters an environment where differences are acknowledged and embraced, creating a vibrant and harmonious community that values each person's unique perspectives and experiences. Here, unity in diversity is a core principle that ensures that everyone, regardless of their background, orientation, or faith, is respected, valued, and celebrated as an integral part of the city's collective identity. In this city, the beauty of inclusivity shines brightly, embodying the ideal that all are welcome, equal, and free to be their authentic selves.

Religious Diversity: A wide range of religious communities coexist in Edmonton, with churches, mosques, synagogues, temples, and other places of worship representing different faiths. This diversity reflects a city's commitment to religious freedom and tolerance.

Newcomers and Refugees: Edmonton has been a destination for newcomers and refugees worldwide. These individuals and families bring their unique backgrounds and cultures, further expanding the city's diversity.

Celebrating and Preserving Cultural Diversity

Edmonton takes great pride in celebrating and preserving cultural diversity through various means. A city's commitment to multiculturalism is evident in numerous cultural festivals, events, and initiatives that promote intercultural understanding and appreciation.

Heritage Festivals: Edmonton hosts a series of heritage festivals throughout the year, such as the Heritage Festival, which showcases culinary delights, art, and traditions of various cultural communities. These festivals allow residents and visitors to immerse themselves in various cultures.

Museums and Cultural Institutions: Edmonton is home to several museums and cultural institutions that exhibit and preserve the history and art of various communities. For instance, the Royal Alberta Museum features indigenous cultures and a history of immigration to Alberta.

Multilingual Resources: The city offers multilingual resources to assist newcomers and promote language diversity. Various community organizations provide language classes, interpretation services, and support for those like me learning English as a Second Language.

Cultural Organizations and Clubs: Edmonton hosts numerous cultural organizations and clubs where members can participate in cultural activities, attend events, and engage with like-minded individuals from their own cultural backgrounds or others.

Art and Performing Arts: Edmonton's artistic community plays a crucial role in showcasing cultural diversity. The city has a thriving art scene, with theatres, galleries, and performance spaces that present a wide range of cultural expressions, including music, dance, and visual art.

Cultural Exchange Programs: Various programs and initiatives promote cultural exchange, allowing residents to experience and learn about different cultures. These programs often involve student exchange, art exhibitions, and cultural demonstrations.

Challenges and Opportunities

While Edmonton's cultural diversity is celebrated and cherished, it is not without challenges. Ensuring that all communities have equal access to opportunities and resources is a continuous effort. Challenges, such as racism, discrimination, and economic disparities, persist and require ongoing attention and action.

Edmonton addressed these challenges by implementing policies and programs promoting inclusivity, equity, and diversity. These efforts aim to create a more inclusive and accepting city for all residents regardless of cultural background.

The city's multiculturalism is not just an abstract concept but a lived reality that I have lived, which enriches the lives of its residents and visitors. Edmonton celebrates its cultural diversity through a myriad of festivals, events, and initiatives, and it continues to grow and evolve as new communities make the city their home.

As Edmonton looks to the future, I believe the city will continue to embrace cultural diversity as one of its greatest strengths. Through preserving and celebrating these cultural traditions, Edmonton stands as an example of how a diverse and inclusive society can flourish and thrive.

Cultural diversity is a significant source of strength and beauty in Edmonton. Here are several ways in which cultural diversity enhances our city:

Cultural Exchange: Different cultures bring unique traditions, languages, art forms, and cuisines to the city. This diversity provides an opportunity for people to learn about and appreciate cultures different from their own, leading to a more vibrant cultural landscape.

Creativity and Innovation: Cultural diversity is a wellspring of creativity and innovation. When people from various backgrounds come together, they bring with them a variety of perspectives and experiences, which leads to fresh ideas and solutions. Edmonton benefits from this diversity in arts, business, and technology fields.

Economic Growth: A diverse population often leads to a diverse economy. A wide range of businesses and services catering to different cultural communities thrive, contributing to economic growth. Additionally, cultural events and festivals attract tourists and boost the local economy.

Social Cohesion: While there may be challenges in achieving social cohesion in a diverse city, it is also a source of strength. By celebrating cultural diversity and promoting inclusion, Edmonton fosters a sense of belonging and unity among its residents.

Enhanced Learning: Educational institutions in Edmonton benefit from cultural diversity as students can learn from and interact with peers from various cultural backgrounds. This exposure leads to a more informed and globally aware population.

Culinary Delights: Cultural diversity often results in a rich culinary landscape. Edmonton boasts a wide array of restaurants and food markets offering delicious dishes from around the world, making it a food lover's paradise.

Art and Culture: Different cultures bring art, music, dance, and traditions to the city. Edmonton showcases a vibrant arts scene with diverse performances and exhibitions that reflect the multifaceted cultural tapestry of the community.

Bridge Building: Cultural diversity bridges different communities, fostering dialogue and understanding among various groups. This leads to more inclusive policies and social initiatives.

Aesthetic Beauty: The aesthetics of Edmonton can also be enhanced through cultural diversity, as the artistic and architectural styles of various cultures influence public spaces and architecture.

Edmonton embraces cultural diversity and promotes inclusivity, mutual respect, and harmony among residents. The city supports and encourages initiatives that celebrate different cultures through festivals, events, and educational programs, creating a dynamic and harmonious community. Choose Edmonton and you will never go wrong.

CHAPTER XI

EDUCATION IS THE KEY TO RESCUE A LIFE OF A YOUNG REFUGEE

Education is crucial for refugees for several reasons and its importance can be even more pronounced in their unique circumstances.

Empowerment and Independence

In a landscape of displacement and conflict, education emerges as a glimmer of hope and a catalyst for changes in the lives of refugees. Education's transformative power is particularly pronounced in terms of empowerment and independence. Education is a crucial vehicle for refugees to take control of their destinies, foster self-reliance, and diminish dependency on support.

Education as an Empowering Force

At its core, education is a powerful agent of empowerment. For refugees, who are often stripped of their homes and familiar surroundings, education becomes a means of regaining control over their lives. Acquiring knowledge and skills empowers them to navigate the challenges of displacement through resilience and determination. It serves as a tool that imparts academic understanding and cultivates a mindset of self-efficacy.

Knowledge as a Key to Self-Reliance

One of the primary ways education empowers refugees is to provide them with tangible skills essential for self-reliance. Whether through vocational training, language acquisition, or basic literacy, education equips refugees with the tools to secure employment and create sustainable livelihoods. This, in turn, reduces their reliance on external aid and charity, allowing them to actively contribute to their own well-being and that of their community.

Breaking Chains of Dependency

Refugees often find themselves trapped in a web of dependence on humanitarian aid. Education is a powerful disruptor of this cycle, breaking the chain of reliance and fostering a sense of autonomy. When refugees acquire skills and knowledge, they gain the ability to meet their own needs, thereby reducing the burden of external assistance. This shift from dependency to self-sufficiency is economically empowering and contributes to a sense of dignity and pride.

Role of Education in Resilience

Displacement brings with it a myriad of practical and emotional challenges. Education plays a crucial role in building resilience in refugees. By providing them with a sense of purpose, structured routine, and tools to overcome obstacles, education becomes a source of strength. It instills in refugees the belief that despite their circumstances, they can shape their futures and overcome adversity.

Education as a Gateway to Opportunities

Beyond immediate empowerment, education opens a world of opportunities for refugees. Children who receive education are better positioned for future success, breaking the cycle of poverty that often accompanies displacement. For adults, vocational training and higher education have paved the way for enhanced employability, improving economic prospects. As refugees integrate into host communities, education bridges social and economic inclusion, offering avenues for meaningful participation.

Empowering Effects on Women and Girls

In many refugee contexts, women and girls face unique challenges, including gender-based violence and limited access to resources. Education has become a powerful tool for empowering women and girls, offering them a chance to break free from traditional roles and societal expectations. By providing education to women, refugees challenge existing gender norms and contribute to creating more inclusive and equitable societies.

Realizing Empowerment Through Education

Examining specific case studies illustrates the tangible impact of education on refugee empowerment. For instance, in refugee camps where educational programs are implemented, there has been a noticeable increase in the number of individuals who actively engage in income-generating activities. When integrated into educational initiatives, vocational training has been shown to equip refugees with marketable skills, enabling them to participate in the local economy.

Furthermore, the long-term effects of education on refugee communities are evident in instances where former refugees, having received an education and returning to their home countries, are positive change agents. These individuals leverage their education to contribute to rebuilding their communities, thereby breaking the displacement cycle and fostering sustainable development.

Challenges and Barriers:

While the transformative potential of refugee education is undeniable, various challenges and barriers persist. Limited access to quality education, language barriers, and inadequate resources in the host countries hinders the effectiveness of educational interventions. Moreover, the psychological trauma experienced by many refugees may affect their ability to engage in the educational process fully.

Addressing these challenges requires a multifaceted approach, including collaboration between governments, non-governmental organizations, and the international community. Investment in education infrastructure, teacher training, and culturally sensitive curricula are essential for creating an enabling environment for refugee education.

Integration and Social Cohesion

In an increasingly interconnected world marked by migration and displacement, the issue of refugee integration has taken center stage. Among the various avenues available to facilitate this integration, schools have emerged as vital bridges that connect refugees with their host communities.

One of the primary challenges refugees face upon arrival in a new country is the language barrier. Schools play a pivotal role in addressing this obstacle by providing language education tailored to refugees' needs. Proficiency in a local language facilitates effective communication and opens doors to academic and professional opportunities. Through language classes and immersion programs, schools have become the nurturing ground for linguistic development, empowering refugees to express themselves and actively participate in the social fabric of their host communities.

Cultural Understanding:

Beyond language, cultural differences can present formidable hurdles for integration. Schools act as incubators of cultural understanding by incorporating diverse perspectives into their curricula. This includes not only the cultural heritage of the host country but also that of refugee students. Educational institutions are spaces where cultural exchange occurs organically, fostering a climate of mutual respect and appreciation. Through exposure to various traditions, customs, and histories, students become equipped with the knowledge to navigate the complexities of their new societal context.

Moreover, schools can organize cultural events, refugee days, festivals, and exchange programs to celebrate diversity and promote cross-cultural interactions. These initiatives extend beyond the classroom, creating an inclusive environment that encourages dialogue and dispels stereotypes. Schools contribute significantly to breaking down cultural barriers and building bridges of understanding by embracing and valuing the rich tapestry of background within the student body.

Building Relationships:

Social cohesion heavily relies on the formation of meaningful relationships within a community. Schools serve as crucibles for forging connections between students, parents, teachers, and the broader local population. In the context of refugee integration, these relationships are essential to creating a supportive network that fosters a sense of belonging. Friendships formed in schools can transcend cultural and linguistic differences and provide a foundation for harmonious coexistence.

Teachers play a crucial role in this process, acting not only as educators but also as mentors and guides. Cultivating an inclusive and empathetic teaching approach promotes a sense of security and trust among students, thereby facilitating their integration into the school community. Additionally, involving parents and a wider community in school activities further strengthens the bonds between refugees and the host society, creating a holistic support system.

Challenges and Solutions

While schools play a vital role in refugee integration, it is essential to acknowledge the challenges they face. Limited resources, overcrowded classrooms, and the need for specialized support for traumatized students are among the hurdles educators must overcome. Adequate training of teachers in cultural competence and trauma-informed practices is crucial to address these challenges effectively.

Furthermore, collaboration among schools, government agencies, NGOs, and local communities is imperative for developing comprehensive integration programs. Initiatives such as mentorship programs, language support services, and extracurricular activities can enhance the overall integration experience of refugees. By pooling resources and expertise, stakeholders can create a more conducive academic and social environment for refugees to thrive.

Psychosocial Support:

During war and different kinds of conflicts, the mental well-being of refugees, particularly children, is often overlooked amidst the urgent concerns of shelter and sustenance. The trauma experienced by displaced individuals can have lasting effects on their psychological health, making psychosocial support an integral component of humanitarian response.

Displacement, whether due to conflict, persecution, or natural disasters, inflicts deep wounds on individuals, leaving a lasting imprint on mental health. The upheaval of fleeing one's home, witnessing violence, and enduring uncertainty about the future can lead to a range of psychological challenges, particularly for vulnerable populations such as children. Anxiety, depression, post-traumatic stress disorder (PTSD), and other mental health issues often become pervasive among those forced to abandon their homes.

Vulnerability of Refugee Children

Displaced children are especially susceptible to the adverse effects of trauma. The disruption of familiar surroundings, separation from family members, and exposure to violence can hinder emotional and cognitive development. The uncertainty of their circumstances exacerbates their vulnerability, making psychosocial support a critical component of addressing their unique needs.

Role of Schools in Providing Structures

Schools have emerged as beacons of hope and stability in the chaotic lives of refugee children. Beyond the conventional role of education, schools offer a structured environment that helps restore the semblance of normalcy. The daily routines of attending classes, interacting with peers, and engaging in educational activities provide a stabilizing force amid upheaval. This structure is fundamental to fostering a sense of security that is essential for the psychosocial well-being of young people.

Establishing a routine within the school setting is a therapeutic tool that aids in the healing process. Routine not only imparts a sense of predictability but also helps in developing coping mechanisms. Predictable schedules allow children to anticipate and navigate their daily lives with a degree of certainty, mitigating anxiety associated with the unpredictability of displacement. By adhering to consistent schedules, schools contribute significantly to refugee children's emotional resilience.

Psychosocial Support in Educational Settings

In addition to the inherent benefits of structure and routine, schools can actively provide psychosocial support tailored to refugee children's needs. Trained educators and support staff play pivotal roles in creating a safe and nurturing environment conducive to emotional healing. Through counselling services, group therapy, and targeted interventions, schools can address psychological scars left by displacement, helping children express their emotions and develop coping mechanisms.

The social aspect is an important therapeutic tool for refugee children. Interacting with peers provides an avenue for emotional expression, mutual support, and developing crucial social skills. Friendships forged in the school environment offer a sense of belonging that counteracts the isolation that displaced individuals often experience. Schools thus become not only centers of learning but also crucial hubs for building a supportive community that is vital for the psychosocial recovery of refugee children.

Cultural Sensitivity and Inclusive Education

Recognizing and respecting the cultural diversity of refugee populations is essential for providing effective psychosocial support. Schools must adopt inclusive educational practices that acknowledge and celebrate the unique backgrounds of their students. Cultural sensitivity fosters a sense of identity and belonging, reinforcing psychosocial support provided by the educational environment.

Future Opportunities:

Access to education can transform the lives of refugees, especially children and young adults, by providing them with essential skills and empowering them to become active contributors to host societies. Education offers a straight light of hope amid the upheaval and uncertainty of displacement, providing a sense of normalcy and stability. It is a vital tool for personal advancement and a means of fostering resilience, building bridges between different cultural contexts, and promoting social justice, human rights, and community development.

However, ensuring widespread access to education for refugees is a challenge. Limited resources, overcrowded camps, and political barriers can hinder efforts to establish and sustain educational programmes. Education is often seen as a secondary concern, overshadowed by more immediate needs, such as food, shelter, and healthcare. It is crucial for the international community to recognize the intrinsic value of education in the context of displacement and allocate resources accordingly.

Refugee education involves comprehensive programs that address the unique needs and challenges displaced populations face. This includes not only formal education but also vocational training and skill development initiatives tailored to the specific contexts and aspirations of refugees. By aligning education with the demands of the job market, refugees become better positioned to secure gainful employment, thus enhancing their economic independence and overall well-being.

Refugee education has profound long-term implications, especially in terms of employment opportunities and economic stability. The skills and knowledge acquired through education have become invaluable assets, opening doors to a myriad of possibilities. Access to quality education ensures that refugees are equipped to navigate the complexities of the job market, thereby breaking the cycle of poverty and dependency that is often accompanied by displacement.

Moreover, education serves as a bridge connecting refugees with the broader society in which they live. By learning the language, customs, and norms of their new surroundings, refugees can integrate more seamlessly and foster mutual understanding and collaboration. Education, therefore, has become a cornerstone for building bridges between different cultural and social contexts.

The impact of education on refugees is not confined to the individual; it radiates outward, influencing families, communities, and societies as a whole. Educated refugees often become agents of positive change, advocating social justice, human rights, and community development. By empowering individuals with the knowledge and skills needed to navigate the world's complexities, education becomes a force that transcends borders and fosters a global community that values inclusivity and diversity.

Preventing a Lost Generation

Refugee children face a challenging predicament in which education becomes a distant dream. This puts them at risk of becoming a "lost generation" with limited opportunities and prospects. However, education has the power to break the cycle of poverty, which often traps families in difficult circumstances. It is key that unlocks doors to a world of possibilities, offering a chance for these young minds to shape their destinies and contribute meaningfully to society.

Without education, refugee children may face significant challenges in securing employment, accessing healthcare, and actively participating in community development. The term "lost generation" highlights the potential loss of human potential and untapped talent that could have been nurtured through learning.

Education equips individuals with the tools they need to navigate the world's complexities, fostering a sense of empowerment and agency. For refugee children, education becomes a source of resilience, allowing them to overcome adversity and envision a future beyond the confines of their circumstances.

Moreover, education acts as a catalyst for social change. By providing refugee children with access to quality education, we invest in their personal development and contribute to the broader goal of creating inclusive and sustainable societies. Educated individuals are more likely to actively engage in community-building activities, advocate social justice, and contribute positively to the economic development of their nations.

In practical terms, education opens up employment opportunities, enabling individuals to break free from the cycle of poverty, which often plagues refugee populations. A well-educated population is better equipped to meaningfully contribute to the workforce, drive innovation, and foster economic growth. This, in turn, creates a ripple effect, uplifting entire communities and paving the way for a brighter, more prosperous future.

The term "lost generation" emphasizes the need for concerted efforts from governments, non-governmental organizations, and the international community to ensure these young minds are not left behind. By investing in refugee education, we invest in the resilience, potential, and future contributions of an entire generation.

Human Rights and Dignity

Education is a crucial human right, particularly for refugees. It is a tool that restores dignity, helps normalize disrupted lives, and rebuilds shattered identities. The Universal Declaration of Human Rights guarantees everyone has a right to education, regardless of their circumstances. Refugees are among the most vulnerable groups globally and providing them with education is not only a benevolent act but also a duty dictated by the recognition of their inherent rights. Education empowers refugees, fosters resilience, and promotes self-determination. It is a stabilizing force that helps them navigate the complexities of their new environments and fosters adaptability.

Education has had a transformative impact on the lives of refugees. It cultivates critical thinking, resilience, and a sense of agency. It also contributes to social cohesion within refugee communities by fostering cultural exchanges and a sense of solidarity. Education breaks the cycle of disadvantages for refugee children and provides an opportunity for upward mobility. Educated refugees often play pivotal roles in the reconstruction of their home countries once stability is restored.

However, numerous challenges impede the realization of this goal. Limited resources, overcrowded refugee camps, language barriers, and discrimination are just a few obstacles that need to be addressed. International collaboration, increased funding, and innovative approaches are imperative to overcome these challenges and to ensure that education remains straight path for refugees worldwide to foresee the future.

Preparation for Return or Resettlement

For those who may eventually return to their home countries or embark on a journey of resettlement in a new location, education has emerged as a powerful tool, equipping them with the essential skills and knowledge needed to navigate the challenges of displacement and forge a brighter future.

Refugees, often forced to flee their homes due to conflict, persecution, or other dire circumstances, face myriad challenges as they grapple with adapting to new environments. In such circumstances, education serves more than just a means of acquiring information; it becomes a lifeline, providing a sense of normalcy, stability, and empowerment. The transformative power of education extends far beyond the classroom, offering refugees the opportunity to develop skills that are not only crucial for their immediate survival but also instrumental in shaping their long-term prospects.

One of the primary benefits of refugee education is the acquisition of language skills. Language serves as a bridge between cultures, fostering communication and connection. Proficiency in the host country's language facilitates day-to-day interactions and opens doors to employment opportunities, social integration, and community engagement. Moreover, language proficiency enables refugees to advocate for their rights, access essential services, and actively participate in the civic lives of their new homes.

Beyond language, education empowers refugees with the knowledge and skills necessary for economic self-sufficiency. Vocational training programs, job readiness courses, and educational initiatives geared towards developing practical skills enable refugees to secure employment and meaningfully contribute to their new communities. By fostering economic independence, education acts as a catalyst for integration, breaking down barriers and dispelling the stereotypes that refugees may encounter.

Education also plays a crucial role in addressing the psychological and emotional tolls of displacement. Trauma from leaving one's home, often under distressing circumstances, can have profound and lasting effects on mental well-being. Schools and educational programs designed with a trauma-informed approach provide a supportive environment for refugees, offering counselling services, psychosocial support, and a sense of community. Education becomes a source of resilience, helping individuals cope with the challenges of displacement and rebuild their sense of identity and purpose.

Moreover, education instills a sense of agency and empowerment in refugees. It goes beyond mere knowledge transfer and nurtures critical thinking, problem-solving skills, and a sense of civic responsibility. In classrooms, refugees can engage in dialogue, share their experiences, and learn from each other, fostering a sense of community and mutual understanding. This not only enhances their personal growth but also contributes to the social cohesion of the broader community.

For refugees who may eventually return to their home countries, education has become a powerful tool for rebuilding shattered societies. The skills and knowledge acquired during their time in exile have become invaluable assets in the reconstruction and development of their homeland. Education has become a catalyst for positive change, equipping individuals with the expertise needed to contribute to nation-building efforts, promote peace, and address the root causes of displacement.

In the context of resettlement, education is a key factor in the successful integration of refugees into new societies. Refugees gain a deeper understanding of the cultural, social, and political dynamics of their host countries through education. This knowledge facilitates smoother integration and contributes to the host community's richness and diversity. Education has become a two-way street, fostering mutual understanding and appreciation between refugees and the host population.

Conflict Prevention:

Conflict is an unfortunate reality that often arises due to misunderstandings, lack of tolerance, and failure to coexist peacefully among diverse communities. However, education has emerged as a powerful tool that can foster a deeper understanding, nurture tolerance, and pave the way for harmonious coexistence.

Consider the plight of refugees–individuals who have been uprooted from their homes due to various forms of turmoil, be it war, persecution, or other crises. These displaced individuals often find themselves grappling with the immediate challenges of survival and the daunting task of rebuilding their lives in unfamiliar environments. In this context, education plays a crucial role in offering academic knowledge and providing a framework for social integration, empathy, and collaboration.

When refugees are provided with access to education, they serve more than just a means of acquiring information; it becomes a gateway to empowerment and a catalyst for sustainable change. Education equips individuals with tools to comprehend and appreciate diverse perspectives, fostering a mindset that is open to dialogue and understanding. By instilling values of tolerance and respect for differences, education lays the foundation for peaceful coexistence among individuals from various cultural, ethnic, and religious backgrounds.

Moreover, the impact of education on conflict prevention extends beyond its immediate context. As refugees gain knowledge and skills, they are better positioned to contribute meaningfully to the societies hosting them. This enhances their prospects for economic self-sufficiency and bolsters the overall resilience and stability of the communities they join. Education, in this sense, becomes a conduit for social cohesion, breaking down barriers and dispelling stereotypes that often fuel intergroup tensions.

The long-term benefits of educating refugees have become apparent in the broader scope of conflict prevention. An educated population is more likely to engage in constructive dialogue, seek non-violent resolution to disputes, and actively participate in democratic processes that underpin stable societies. By addressing the root causes of conflict—ignorance, fear, and prejudice—education becomes a proactive force in building a future where differences are celebrated rather than feared.

In essence, the role of education in conflict prevention is not just about imparting knowledge; it is also about nurturing the human spirit, fostering empathy, and sowing the seeds of peace. It is a powerful investment in the collective well-being of societies, transcending immediate challenges to shape a more harmonious and resilient world for future generations.

Health and Well-being:

Educational institutions play an irreplaceable role in the health and well-being of refugee children. These schools impart academic education and serve as gateways to essential healthcare services, providing central support for the diverse health needs of the young individuals they serve.

Regular attendance of refugee children at these schools is not only an academic obligation but also a means of meticulously observing and attending to their health concerns.

With its structured schedule and regular interactions, the school environment has become a dynamic platform for monitoring and addressing various health issues that may arise among students.

Schools are more than just centers of learning; they transform into nurturing spaces that actively contribute to the holistic well-being of refugee children. By providing access to healthcare services and establishing a system for vigilant health oversight, these educational institutions become integral partners in safeguarding and enhancing the health of young people within their care.

Cultural Preservation:

Cultural preservation is crucial in schools, as it helps to create a sense of identity and belonging for refugees while ensuring that their rich cultural heritage is not only acknowledged but also celebrated. By integrating elements of refugees' culture into the curriculum, educational institutions can create an inclusive learning environment beyond just academic instruction.

Incorporating cultural elements into the curriculum is not enough to teach traditional customs and practices. This involves infusing diverse perspectives, histories, and languages into various subjects. For instance, literature classes can explore works from refugees' cultural backgrounds, allowing students to appreciate and understand different storytelling traditions. Similarly, history lessons can include a comprehensive examination of refugee heritage, highlighting its contributions and historical significance.

Extracurricular activities and cultural events also play vital roles in showcasing and preserving diverse cultures. Organizing multicultural festivals, art exhibitions, and music performances can be powerful tools for fostering cross-cultural understanding and appreciation within the school community. These events contribute to preserving refugees' cultural identity and encourage a sense of pride and unity among students.

Collaboration with the local community and cultural organizations further enhances the effectiveness of cultural preservation efforts. Inviting guest speakers, arranging field trips to culturally significant sites, and establishing partnerships with community leaders can provide valuable insights and practical experiences that enrich the educational journey.

A Heartfelt Appreciation To My Mentors At UNHCR Solwezi

Dear Mentors,

I hope this letter finds you in good health and high spirits. As I sit down to pen these words, a flood of emotions overwhelms me, and I find it challenging to express the depth of my gratitude and admiration for the profound impact you both have had on my life.

Firstly, I want to convey how much I miss the vibrant atmosphere of the UNHCR offices in Solwezi and Meheba. The memories of our shared experiences, the camaraderie, and the sense of purpose we cultivated together remain etched in my heart. The time I spent under your guidance, both as a refugee and Child and youth care worker (CYCW), has become an invaluable chapter in my life, shaping the person I am today.

Your strong dedication to the cause of humanitarian work has been nothing short of inspiring. Witnessing your tireless efforts to make a positive difference in the lives of refugees and displaced individuals has left an indelible mark on my soul. The resilience and compassion with which you approached every challenge became a beacon of light, guiding me through my own journey in the humanitarian field.

I want to express my deepest appreciation for the wealth of knowledge and skills you imparted to me during our time together. Your mentorship not only equipped me with the practical tools needed for this demanding line of work but also instilled in me a profound sense of responsibility and empathy. The lessons learned from you have become the bedrock of my approach to humanitarian service.

It brings me immense joy to share with you that I am currently engaged in humanitarian work, a path I embarked upon with the invaluable lessons learned under your tutelage. Your teachings have become the compass that guides my actions, and I am honoured to carry forward the torch of compassion and commitment that you so passionately ignited within me.

In moments of doubt or challenge, I often find myself reflecting on the examples you set and the encouragement you provided. Your mentorship has not only shaped my professional journey but has also influenced the very core of my character. I am profoundly grateful to have been mentored by such exceptional individuals from Solwezi and Meheba UNHCR offices.

As I navigate the challenges of the humanitarian field, I carry the lessons from Solwezi and Meheba with me like a cherished treasure. I want you both to know that your impact reaches far beyond the confines of those offices—it reverberates in the lives you've touched and the positive change you've inspired.

In closing, please accept my heartfelt thanks for being the guiding light in my life. I look forward to the day when our paths cross again, and I can express my gratitude in person. Until then, please know that you are always in my thoughts, and the impact of your mentorship resonates in every endeavour I undertake.

With deepest appreciation and warm regards,
Bazibuhe Muhabwa

REFERENCES

Humanium. (2021). Children of the Democratic Republic of the Congo https://enoughproject.org/blog/congo-first-and-second-wars-1996-2003

https://www.humanium.org/en/democratic-republic-congo/

World Atlas, (2021). What are the Major Natural Resources of the Republic of the Congo?

https://www.worldatlas.com/articles/what-are-the-major-natural-resources-of-the-republic-of-the-congo.html

Manufactured by Amazon.ca
Bolton, ON

46228942R00131